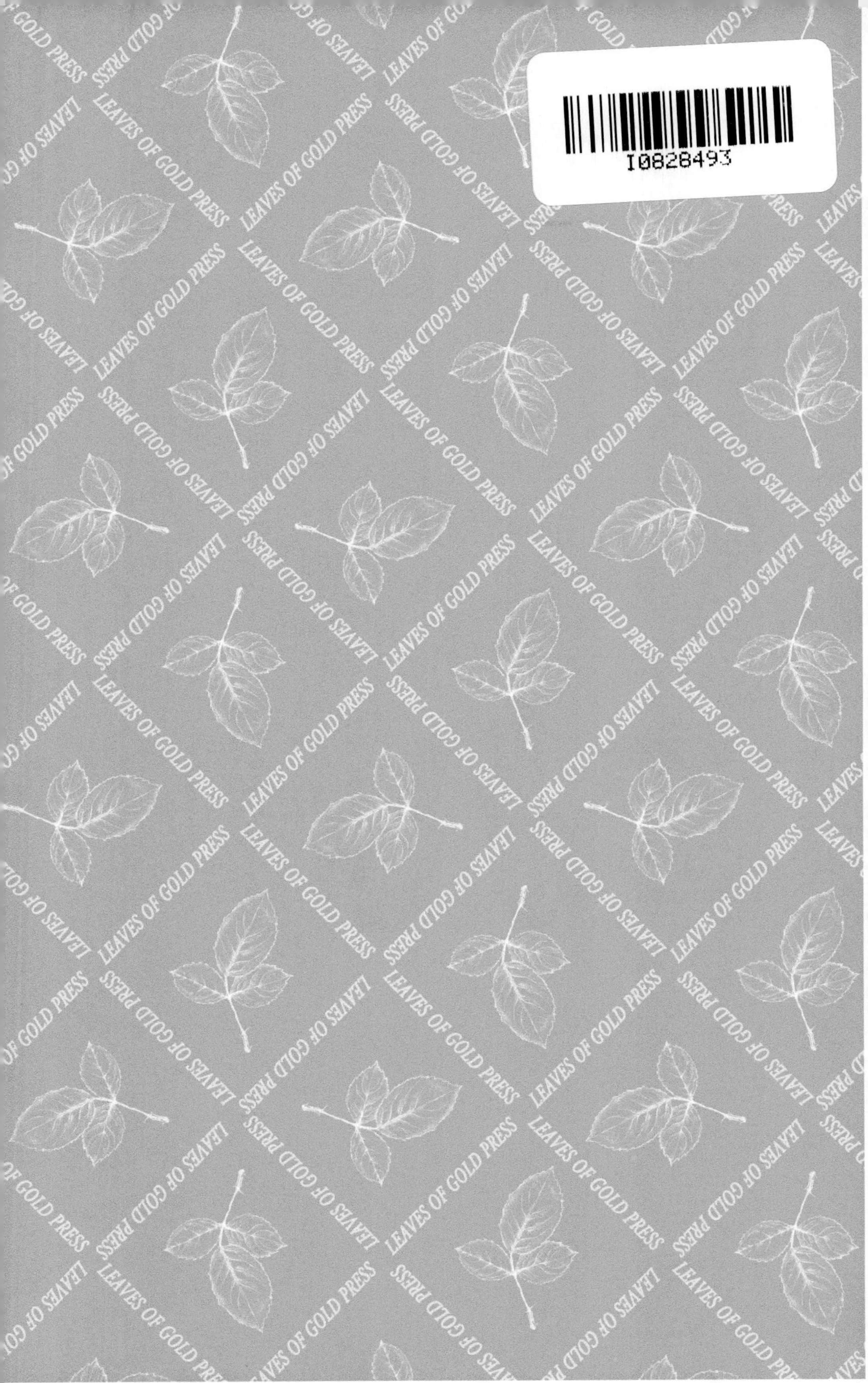
LEAVES OF GOLD PRESS
I0828493

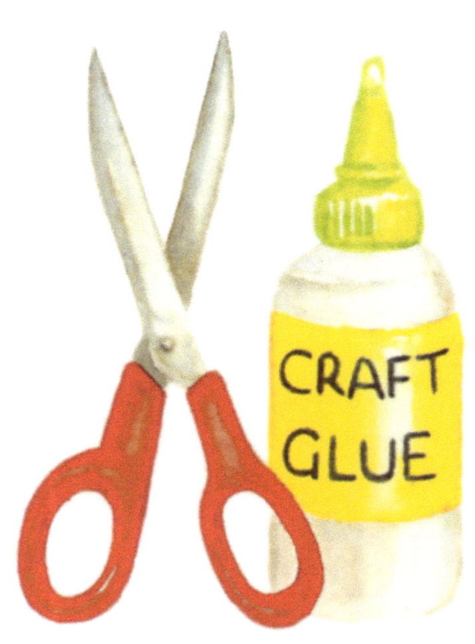
CRAFT
GLUE

The 'Parents' Time Off' Series

KIDS' CREATIVE CRAFT ACTIVITIES

Cecilia Egan
Illustrated by Christine Eddy

First published in 1990 by Ashton Egan
as The Kids' First Book of Craft Activities

Revised and updated 2015

National Library of Australia Cataloguing-in-Publication entry

Creator: Egan, Cecilia, author.
Title: Kids' creative craft activities / Cecilia Egan ;
Christine Eddy, illustrator.

Edition: 2nd edition
ISBN: 9781925110739 (paperback)
Series: Parents' time off series ; 6.
Target Audience: For primary school age (6-12 year old)

Subjects: Creative activities and seat work.
Handicraft for children.
Handicraft--Juvenile literature.

Other Creators/Contributors: Eddy, Christine, illustrator.

Dewey Number: 745.5083

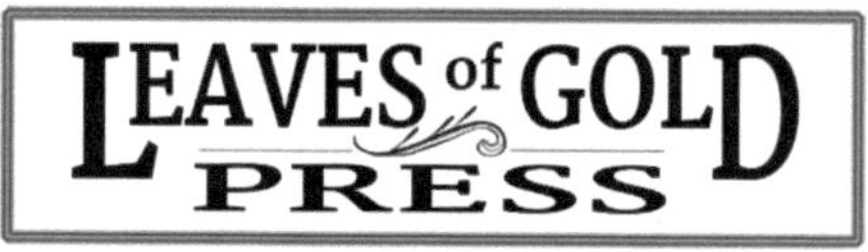

ABN 67 099 575 078

PO Box 9113, Brighton, 3186, Victoria, Australia
www.leavesofgoldpress.com

INTRODUCTION

Kids' Creative Craft Activities provides hours of creative fun for pre-schoolers and older children, using materials which are easily obtained.

These materials are written in **bold type** so that you know at a glance what you will need.

Activities are graded with star symbols:
*   Very easy
** Easy
*** For older children

This beautifully illustrated book will delight every family!

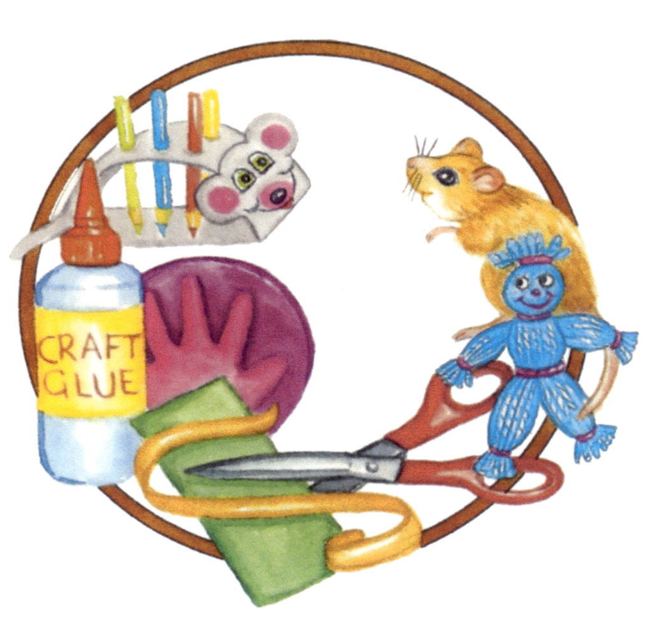
CRAFT
GLUE

CONTENTS

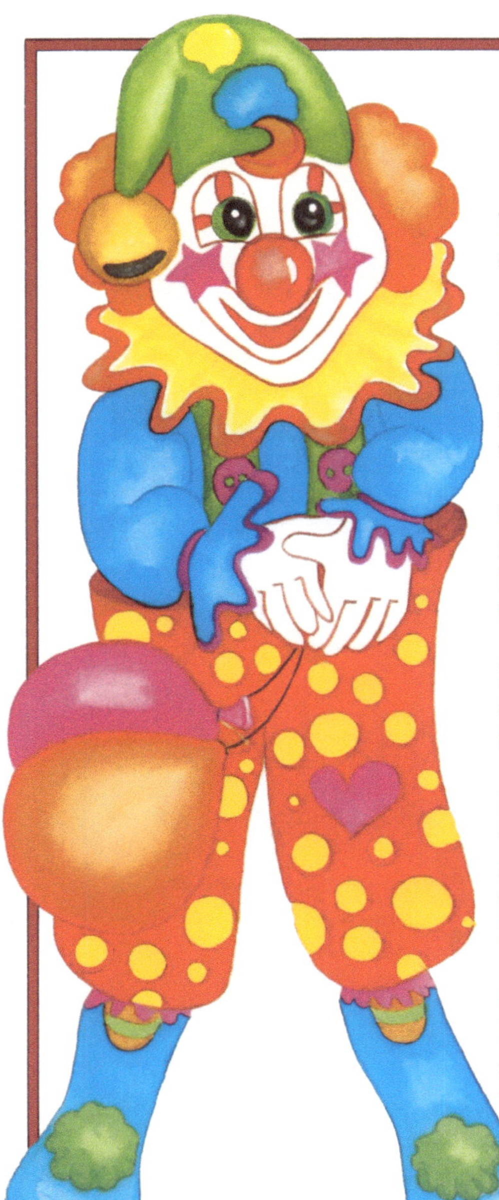

CLOWN FINGER PUPPET *

This walking clown is easy to make.

1. Trace this clown onto light **cardboard** or make up your own clown. Cut around the shape with **scissors**.

Colour in the clown with **markers** or **poster paints.** Bend the feet forwards so they stand flat.

2. Cut two strips of **paper** about 2 cm (1 inch) wide by 7 cm (3 inches) long.

Roll them into tubes that fit your fingers. **Glue** the ends down and glue the tubes to the backs of the legs.

Put your fingers into the tubes and make the clown walk.

POTATO FAMILIES*

You can make a potato family or even a royal family with some scraps from around the house. Collect a large, medium and small potato.

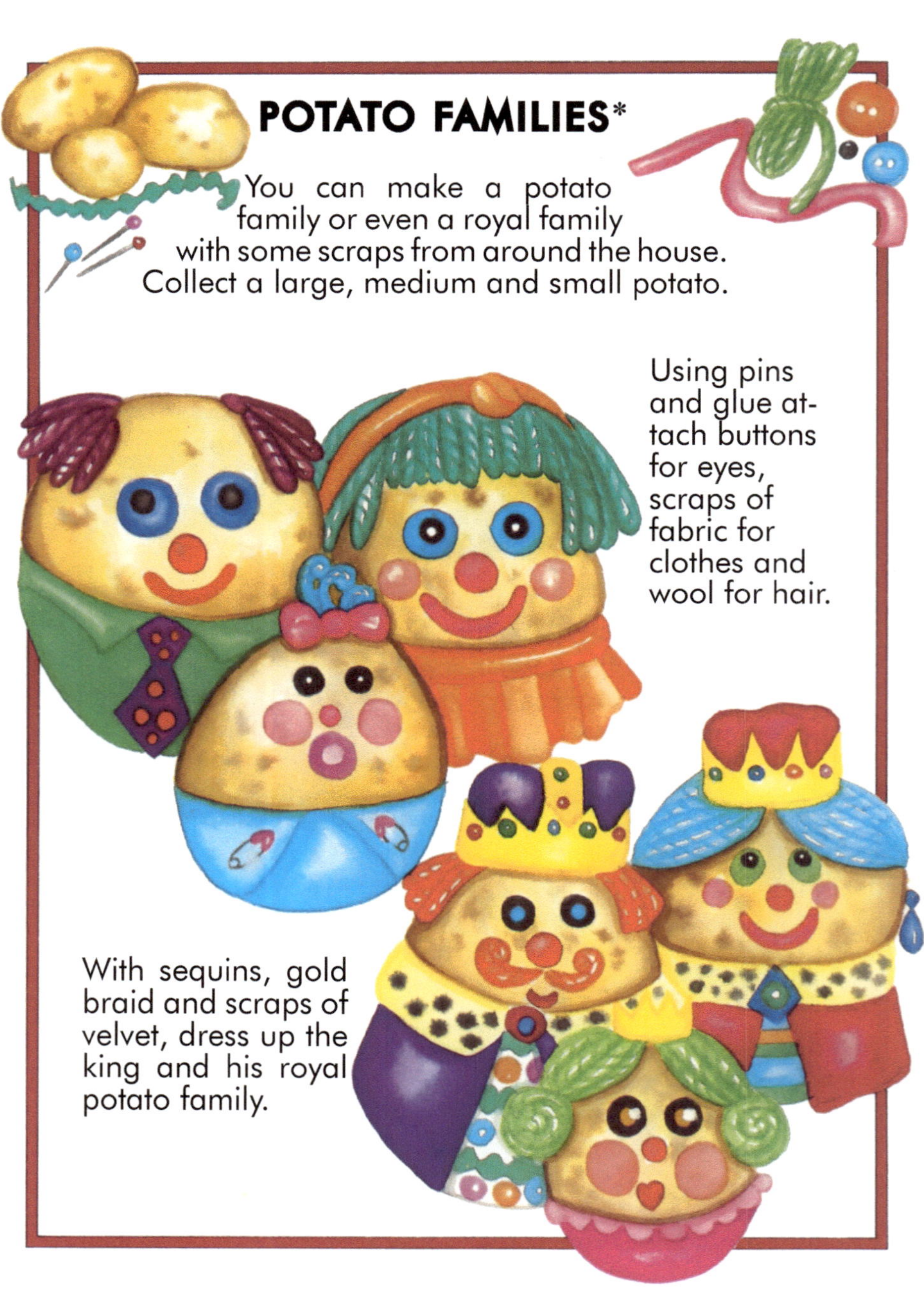

Using pins and glue attach buttons for eyes, scraps of fabric for clothes and wool for hair.

With sequins, gold braid and scraps of velvet, dress up the king and his royal potato family.

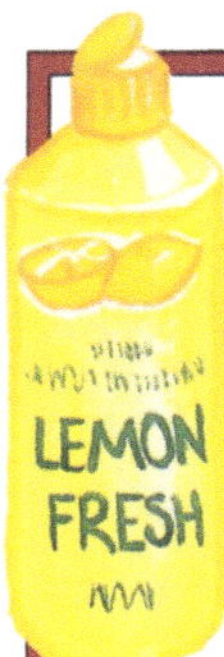

PAINTED SQUIRTERS*

Have fun out of doors with these squirters, but make sure you are wearing old clothes.

1. Pull off or unscrew the top nozzles of two empty dishwashing liquid bottles (one for you and one for your friend). Wash the bottles inside and out. Leave them to dry.

2. Paint the bottles with acrylic paints and a paint brush. Let the paint dry.

3. Fill the bottles with water, and replace the squirter nozzles.

Stand back-to-back with a friend, each of you holding a bottle squirter in both hands. Slowly walk three paces forward, turn and squeeze!

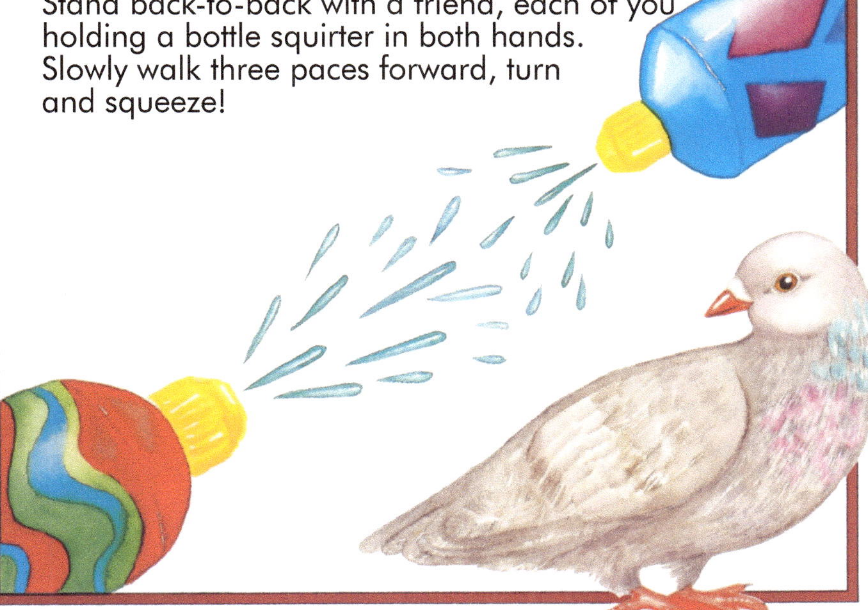

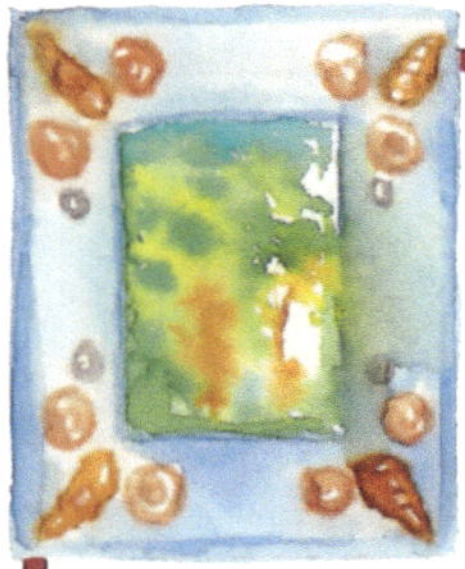

DECORATIVE SHELLS*

It is fun to collect different sorts of shells on your holidays.

Use sand and shells to decorate boxes, mirrors, picture frames, garden pots, jars and haircombs. Never take shells that have animals living inside them.

1. Wash and scrub the shells thoroughly using an old nail brush or toothbrush.

2. To make a decorative container coat a flower pot or jar with strong glue. Cover the outside of the container with sand. Shake off the loose sand when the glue is dry.

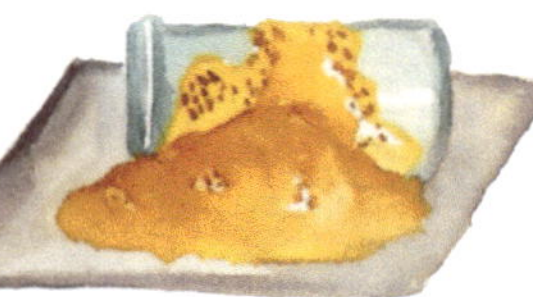

Decorate by glueing on the shells in waves and bands and pleasing patterns.

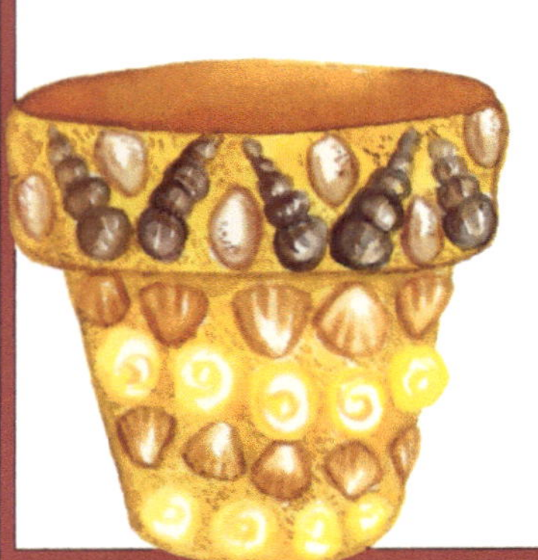

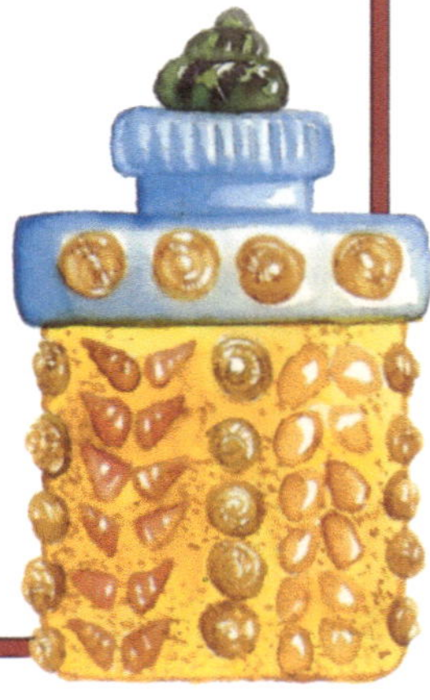

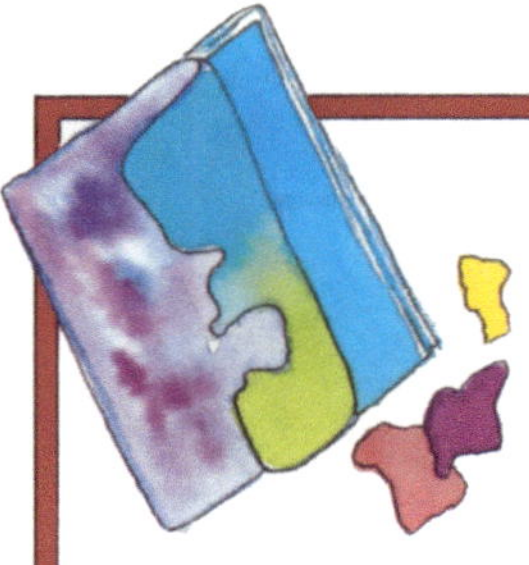

MAGAZINE COLLAGE*

You can make a lovely picture by using torn or cut pieces of coloured paper.

Look through some old magazines and tear out areas which have plain patches of colour.
Roughly outline your picture with pencil onto a sheet of paper. Keep in mind the light and dark areas in your picture. For shadows use darker shades of the same colour.
Glue the pieces of coloured paper onto your paper to form your collage.

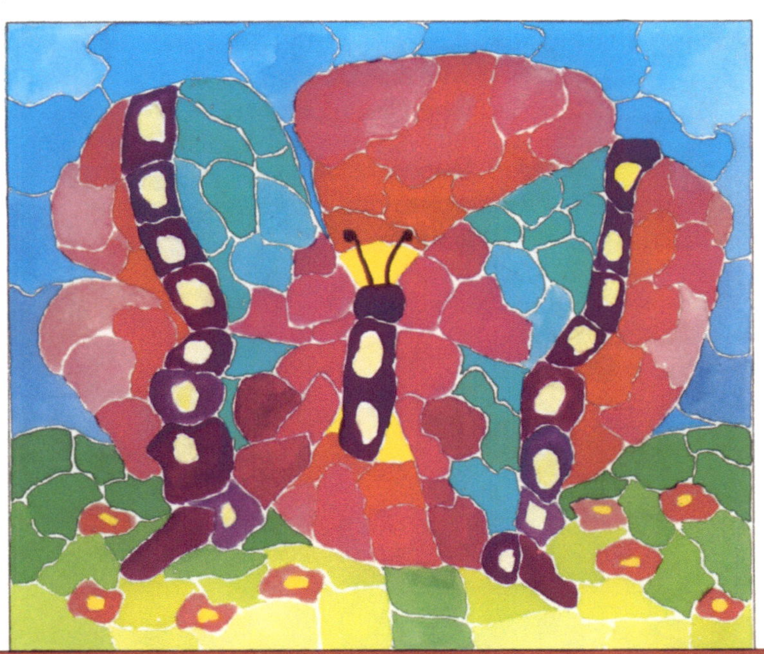

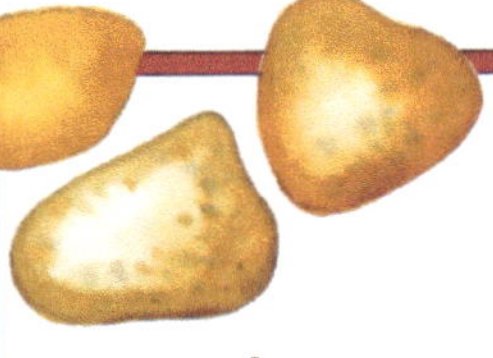

STONE PAPER-WEIGHT*

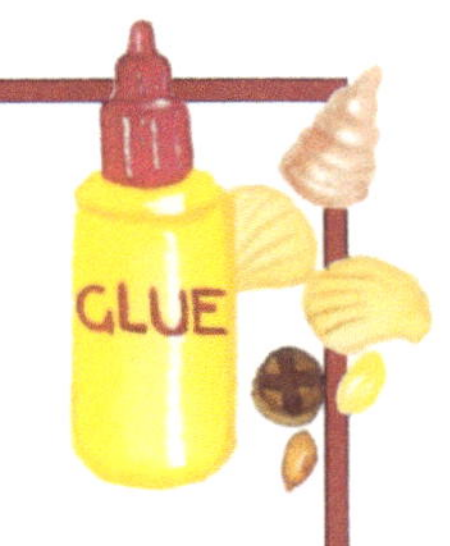

Transform any large, smooth stones you find into decorative paper-weights.

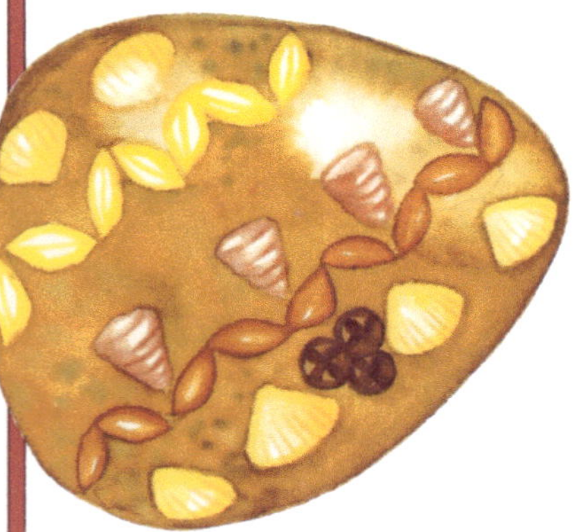

1. Make sure that the stone is clean and dry. Choose small, attractive beads, seeds and shells and glue them to the stone. Use a strong glue.

Work out your pattern on a piece of paper before you start glueing.

2. You can also paint pictures or patterns onto your stones with poster paints. The shape of your stone may give you an idea.

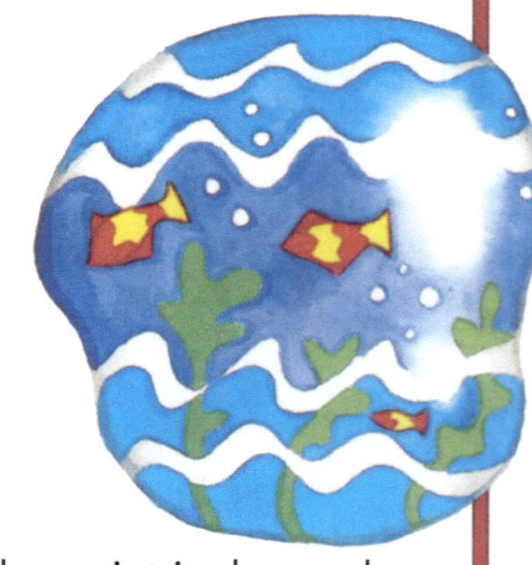

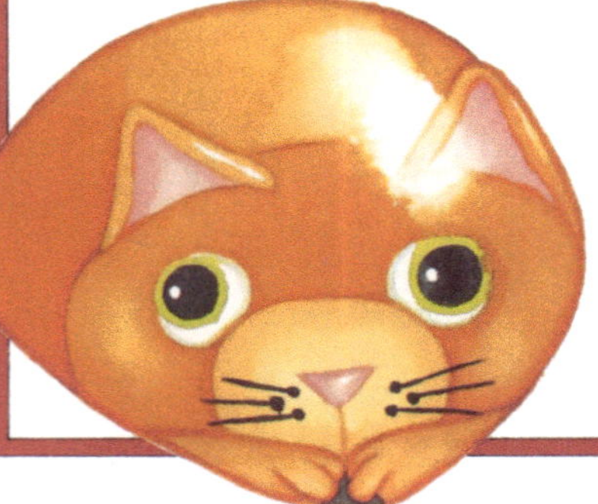

When the paint is dry, make your stones shiny by painting on polyurethane varnish with a brush.

MEMENTO BASKET*

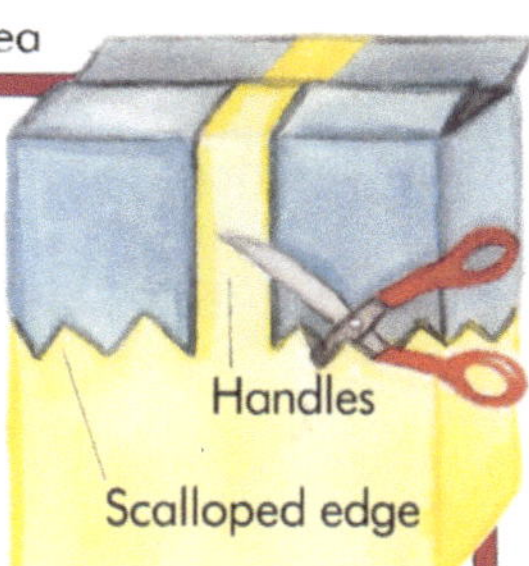

Mementos are little treasures you keep to remind you of special occasions or people in your life.

They may include photos, letters, cards, theatre tickets, brochures from art galleries and museums, pressed leaves and flowers from nature walks, menus, invitations or party favours. Make this memento basket to keep them in.

1. Cover a cereal box with plain paper and glue it on. Draw a scalloped line around the box as shown above, right.

2. With scissors cut away the shaded area, leaving handles as shown. Glue the handles together at the top.

3. Use poster paints to decorate your basket.

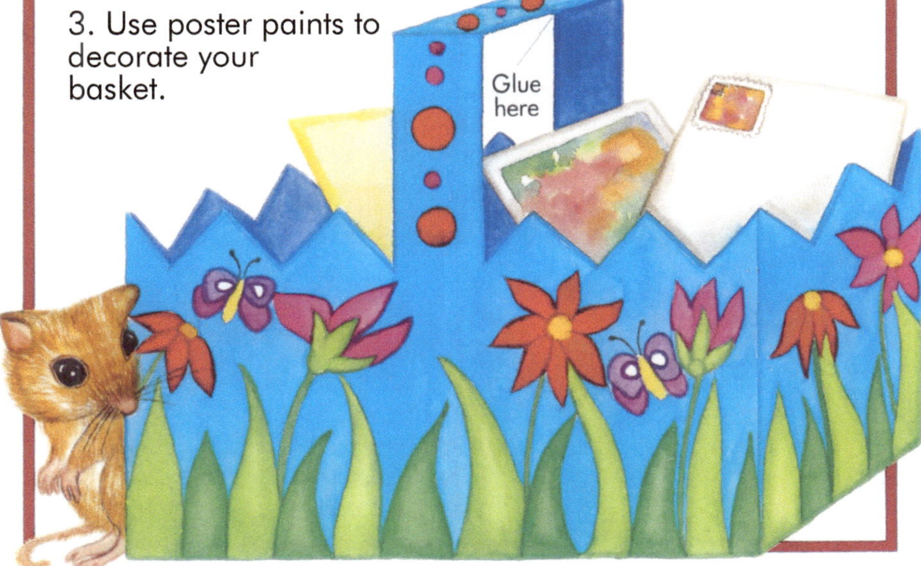

PAPER PLATE MASKS*

You can transform yourself into a different character or animal using just a **paper plate, paints and decorative scraps**.

1. Using **scissors** cut a triangle for a nose hole in the centre of the plate. Cut two circles for eye holes.

2. Use **acrylic paints and a brush** to create a face. Let your imagination go!

3. Decorate your mask with any kinds of scraps you can find, e.g. **pipe cleaners** for whiskers, **wool and crepe paper strips** for hair or fur, **cotton balls** for sheep's wool, **curling ribbon, cardboard**.

4. Make a hole on each side, near the edges of the plate, using the point of your scissors. Loop **elastic bands** through the holes, shown on the plate at the top of the page on the right. Slip the loops over your ears and you are transformed!

BREAD BEAD NECKLACE*

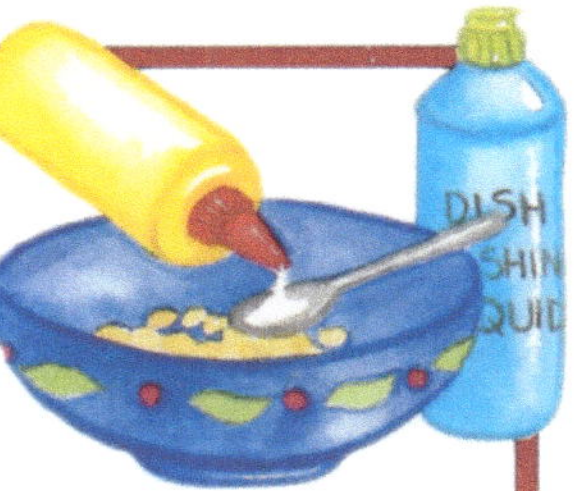

Make these brightly coloured beads to wear.

1. Crumble **three crust-less slices of bread** in **a bowl.**

2. Add three teaspoons of **glue** and three drops of **washing-up liquid.**
Mix into a smooth dough, adding a little **water** if necessary.

3. Roll small pieces of dough into balls and push them onto **a fine knitting needle.**

Leave them to dry in a warm place to dry for about 24 hours.

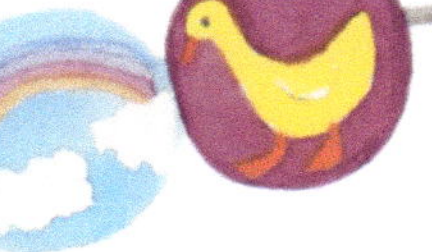

4. When the beads are dry, colour them with **acrylic paints and a brush.** Thread them onto **shirring elastic** to make a necklace or bracelet.

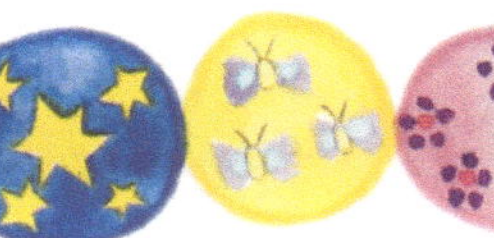

EGGS-TREMELY PRETTY**

Make an unusual decorated egg shell.

1. Place a raw **egg** in an **egg-cup** and gently pierce a hole in one end with a d**arning needle**. Turn it over and pierce a slightly larger hole in the other end.

2. Hold the egg over a **bowl** and gently blow into the smaller hole until the soft parts come out of the other end. (Save the inner egg for someone to cook with later.)

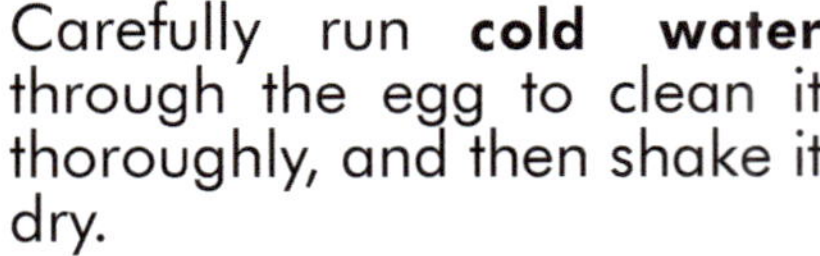

Carefully run **cold water** through the egg to clean it thoroughly, and then shake it dry.

You might like to use **poster paints** to colour your egg before you decorate it.

3. Coat half the egg with **strong glue**.

4. Stick on **braid, wool, beads, sequins or seeds**.

Let the glue dry then turn it over and decorate the other half.

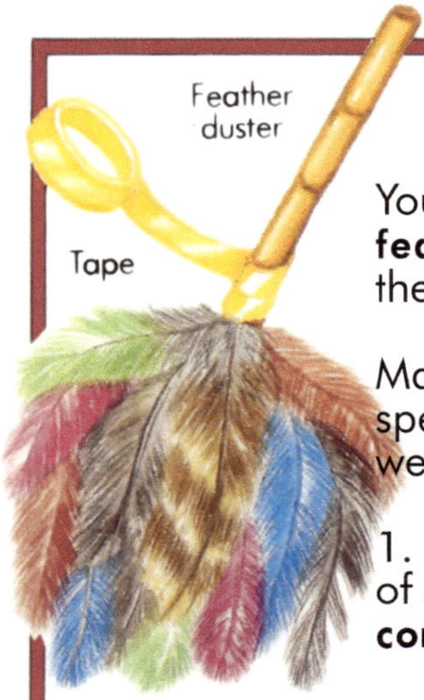

Feather duster

Tape

FESTIVE FEATHERS**

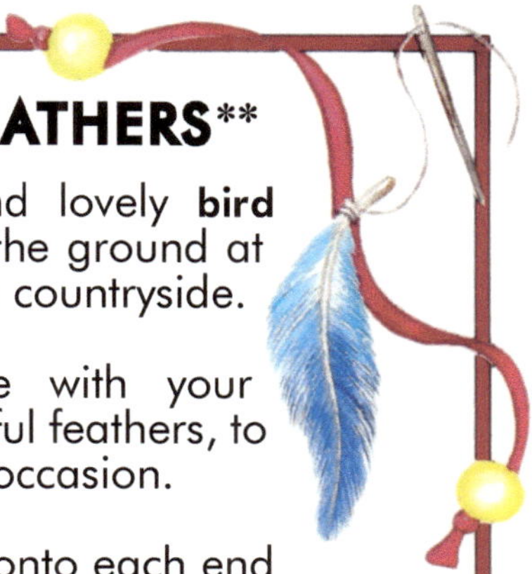

You can often find lovely **bird feathers** lying on the ground at the beach or in the countryside.

Make a necklace with your special and colourful feathers, to wear on a special occasion.

1. Thread a **bead** onto each end of some short pieces of **ribbon or cord.** Knot the ends.

2. Use a a **threaded needle to** sew one feather onto the end of each piece of ribbon or cord as shown above.

3. Have **a longer and wider piece of ribbon**, 30 cm (12 inches) long. Put a bead on each end and tie a knot.

4. Tie all the short pieces of ribbon onto the longer ribbon and make into bows.

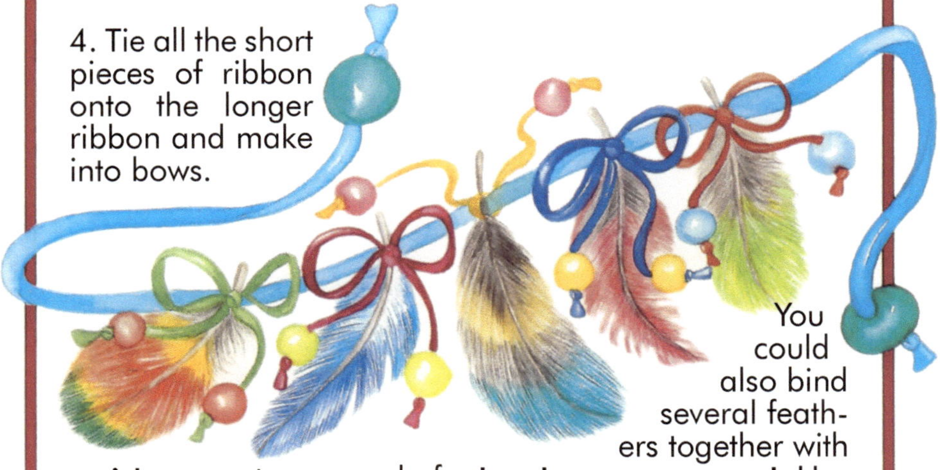

You could also bind several feathers together with **sticky tape** to one end of a **bamboo or cane rod**. Use your feather duster to help clean the house.

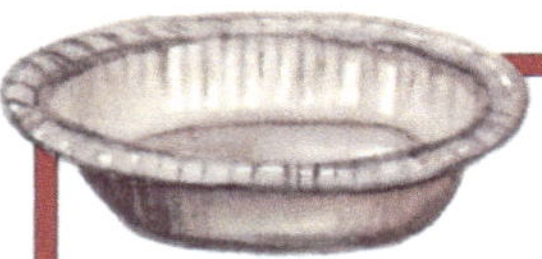

PLASTER CASTS**

Make this plaster cast of your hand as a memento for Mum or Dad. A friend can make one with you.

1. Mix **plaster of Paris** with water until it is smooth and stiff. Pour the plaster into a **foil pie dish**.

2. Press your hand into the plaster. Keep your hand still until you feel the plaster begin to set.

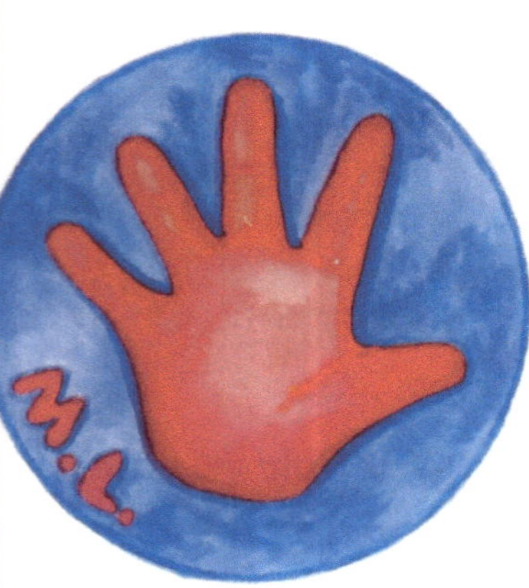

3. Remove your hand gently when you can take it away without taking plaster too. Scratch your initials into the plaster with the rounded end of a **brush**.

4. When the plaster is completely dry turn the plaster out of the dish. Paint the cast with **acrylic or poster paints**.

5. You can make impressions of other obiects too, such as **shells, seed pods and fruit**.

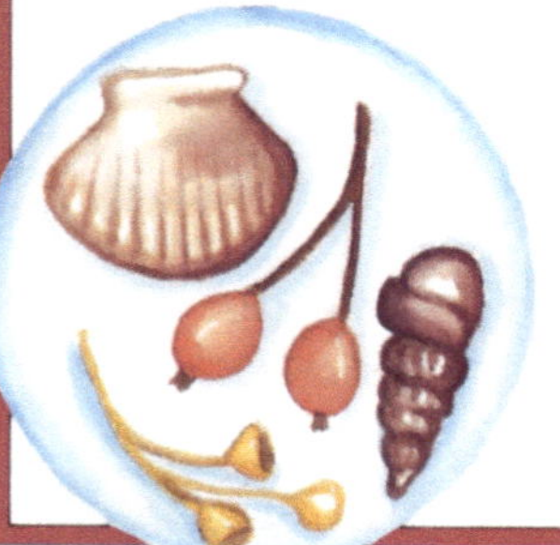

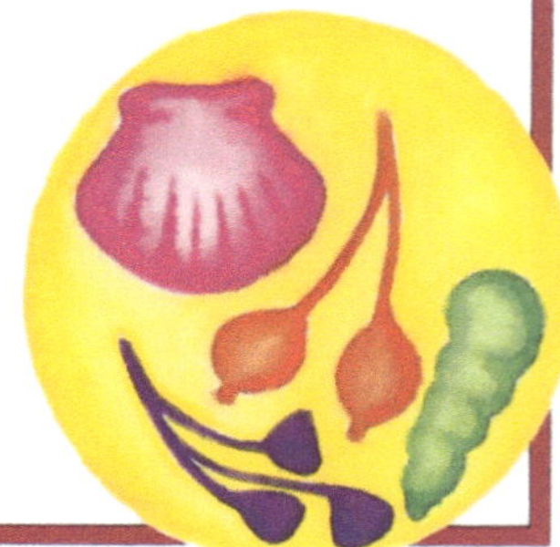

STICKER APRON***

There are many types of stickers. Some are for advertising purposes, some carry a message and others are decorative.

You might be able to get some free **stickers** if you ask politely at places like shops, gas stations or travel agencies. Explain that you are collecting stickers.

You can use your stickers to decorate books or an apron. An apron is useful for keeping your clothes clean while you are doing other craft activities, or you could give it as a gift.

Use **scissors** to cut out this apron shape, from **plastic-coated cloth**. (It doesn't need to be hemmed.) Cut two long pieces of **tape** to make apron ties and a short one for around the neck.

Sew the tapes to the apron with **a needle and thread.**

Decorate the apron with your stickers; they stick easily.

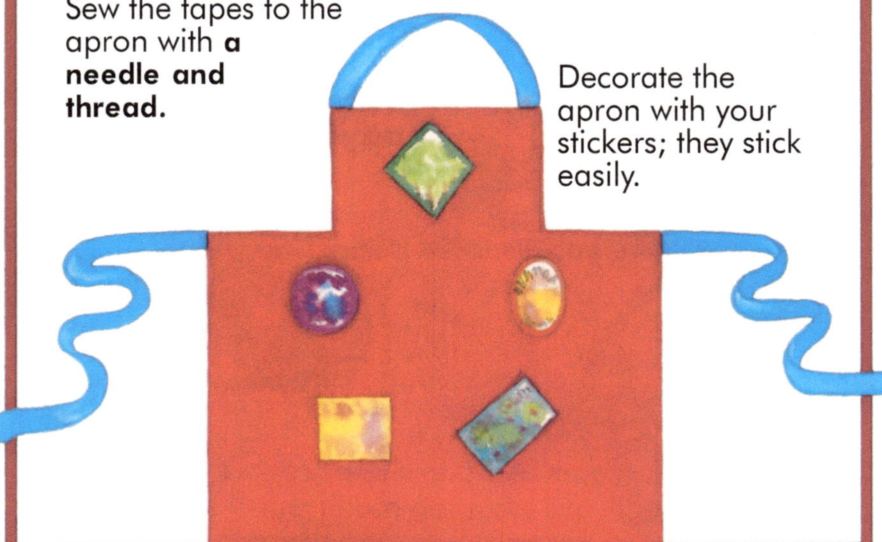

WOOL DOLLS***

Make these dolls from **wool.** You can make them in your favourite team colours too.

1. Wind thick wool around the length of a **postcard**. Slip the wool off the card. Tie the bundle in two places near the top with short lengths of wool to make the face.

2. With **scissors** cut through all the loops at the top and at the bottom. Wind more wool around the width of the post-card to make the arms. Slip the wool off the card and tie each end of the bundle. Snip through the loops and push the arms through the centre of the body.

3. Tie a piece of wool just under the arms to make the waist. Divide the bundle in half to make legs.
Tie each near the end.

4. Give your doll a face by sewing or **glueing** on **buttons, sequins or pieces of felt.**

Use a longer piece of card if you want to give your doll long hair that you can style.

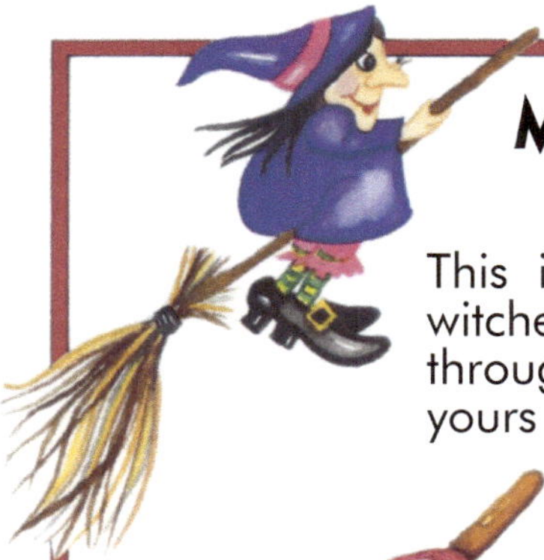

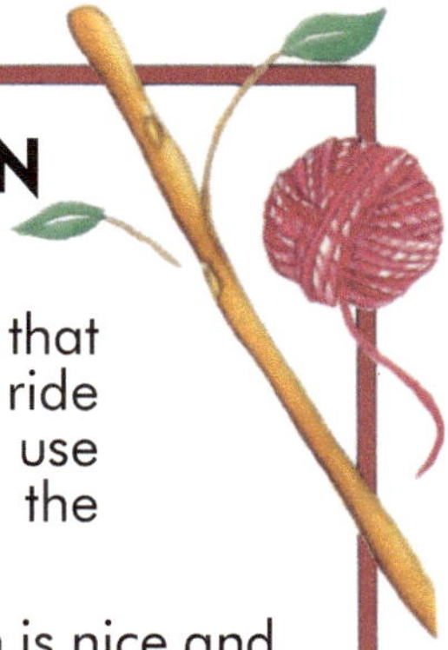

MAKE YOUR OWN BROOM*

This is the sort of broom that witches in fairytales use to ride through the skies! You can use yours for sweeping away the leaves.

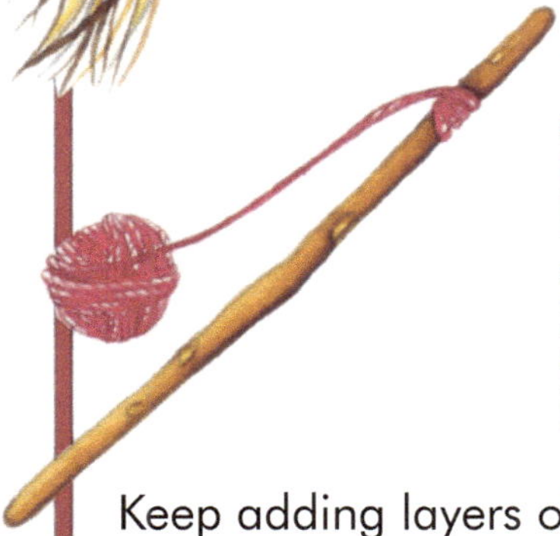

1. Find **a branch** which is nice and straight, about 1.5 metres long. Bind some **strong string** to the branch, 20 cm (8 inches) from one end.
2. Tie your first layer of **long, tapering twigs** to the branch, binding them tightly as you go.

Keep adding layers of twigs until your broom is thick.

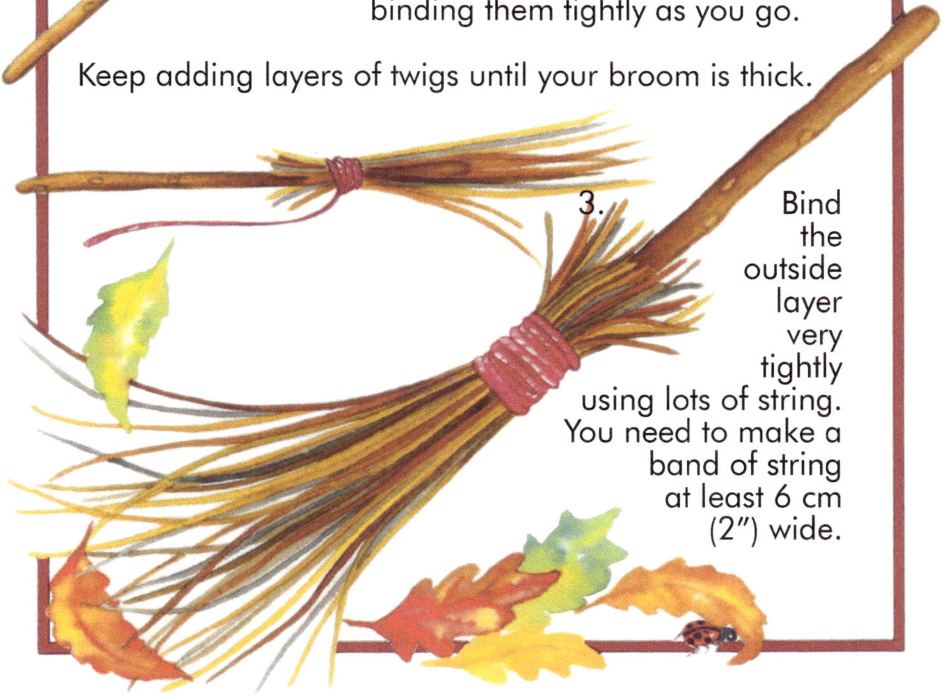

3. Bind the outside layer very tightly using lots of string. You need to make a band of string at least 6 cm (2″) wide.

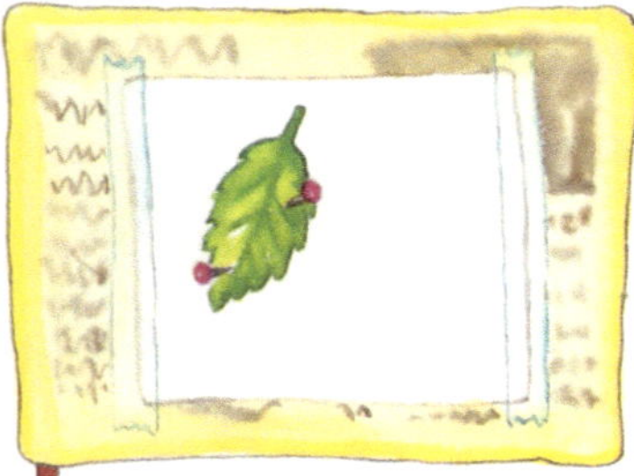

SPATTER PAINTINGS*

This activity can be messy so wear an apron (the 'sticker apron' would be ideal).

1. Spread out several sheets of **newspaper**. Tape **a sheet of white or coloured paper** on these, so it won't move.

2. Use **small pins** to fix **a leaf, cut out paper shape or any other flat shape**, onto your sheet of paper. Make sure there is a thick wad of newspaper under this so that the pins don't mark the table.

Mix some **poster paint** with a little **water** but don't make it too runny. Put different colours in separate **saucers**.
Dip **an old toothbrush** into one of the paint colours.

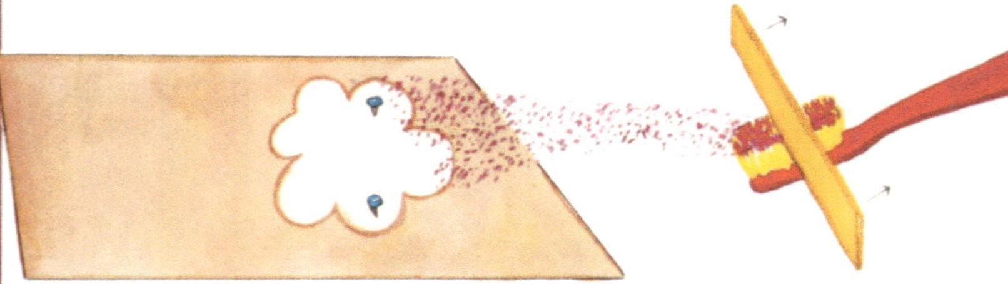

Using the edge of **an oblong piece of cardboard**, move it across the top of the toothbrush bristles towards you.
If you move the cardboard away from you, you will be the one covered with paint! Hold the brush towards the paper and the paint will spatter across the paper.

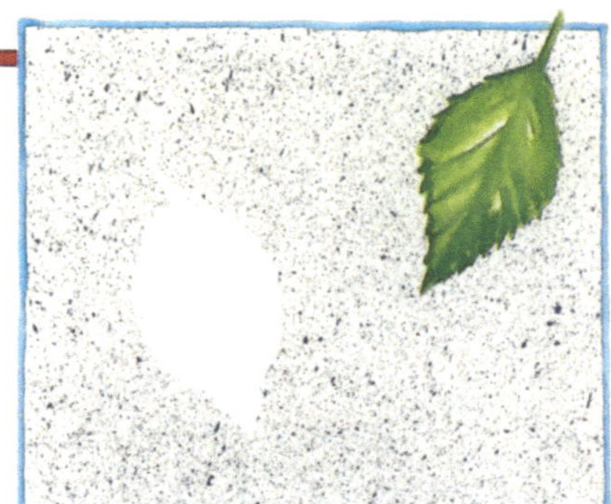

When the paper is spattered all over, wait for a few minutes to let the paint dry a little before lifting off the leaf.

3. Pin a second leaf onto the paper, overlapping the first shape slightly.

Clean your brush in a jar of water and use another colour to again spatter the paper.

You can repeat the above steps with several other colours but do not spatter too heavily or too often or the painting will be messy.

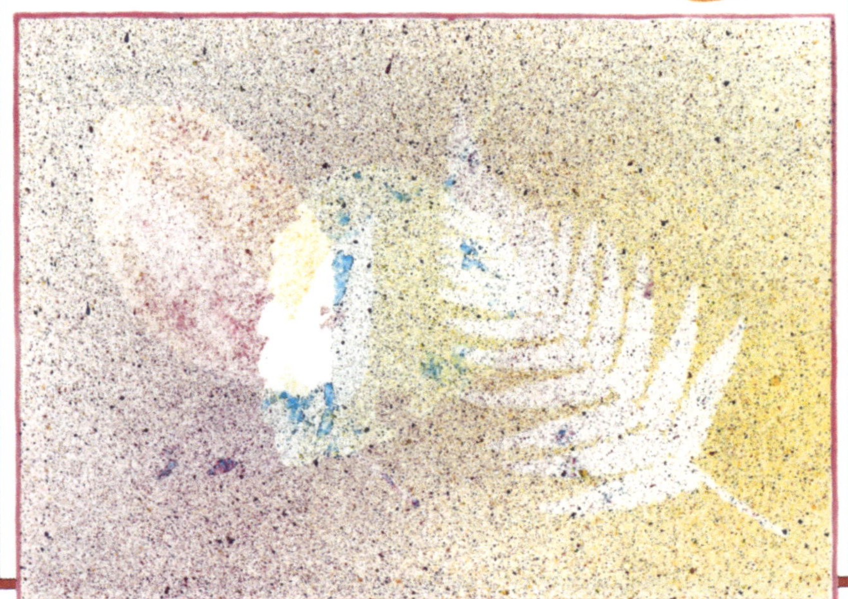

MOUSE TIDY***

This mouse tidy will hold your pencils, keeping them tidy and ready to use.

1. With a **pencil**, trace the pattern below onto **a sheet of cardboard**.
It should measure 324 mm (12.7 inches) long by 75 mm (2.9 inches) wide.

2. Cut out the shape with **scissors**. Carefully use a **utility knife** (get an adult to help) and cut around the solid outline of the tail (not the dotted line). Make criss cross cuts in the mouse's back. This is where the pencils will go.

3. Colour the mouse with **paints or markers**.

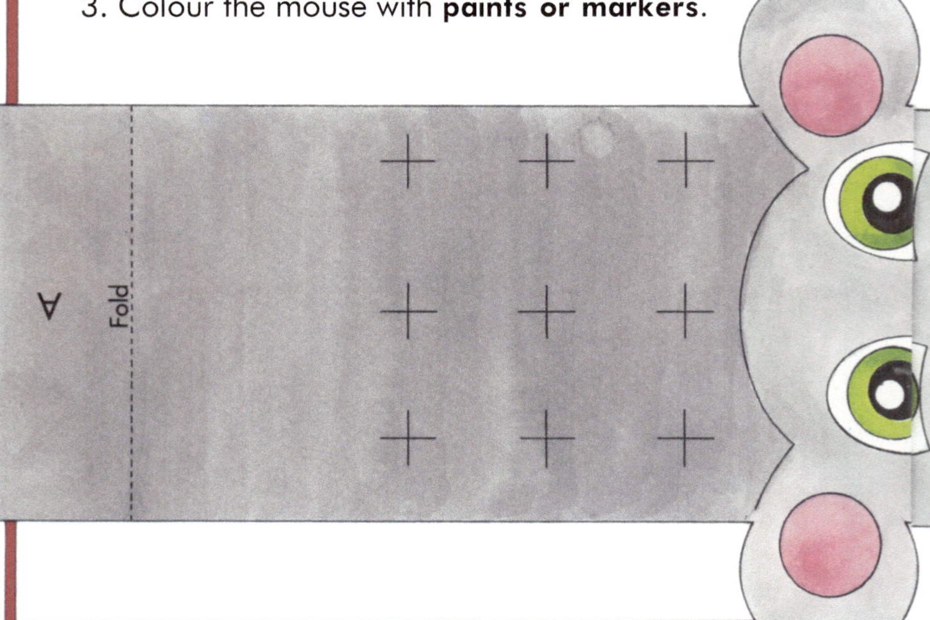

4. Fold along the dotted lines. Bend the tail out as shown so that it is sticking out from the back of the mouse.

5 Bend the card shape around and **glue** the flap marked 'A' in under the tail end of the mouse.

6. You can use **coloured round sticky labels** for the eyes or trace the face from the pattern and colour it in.

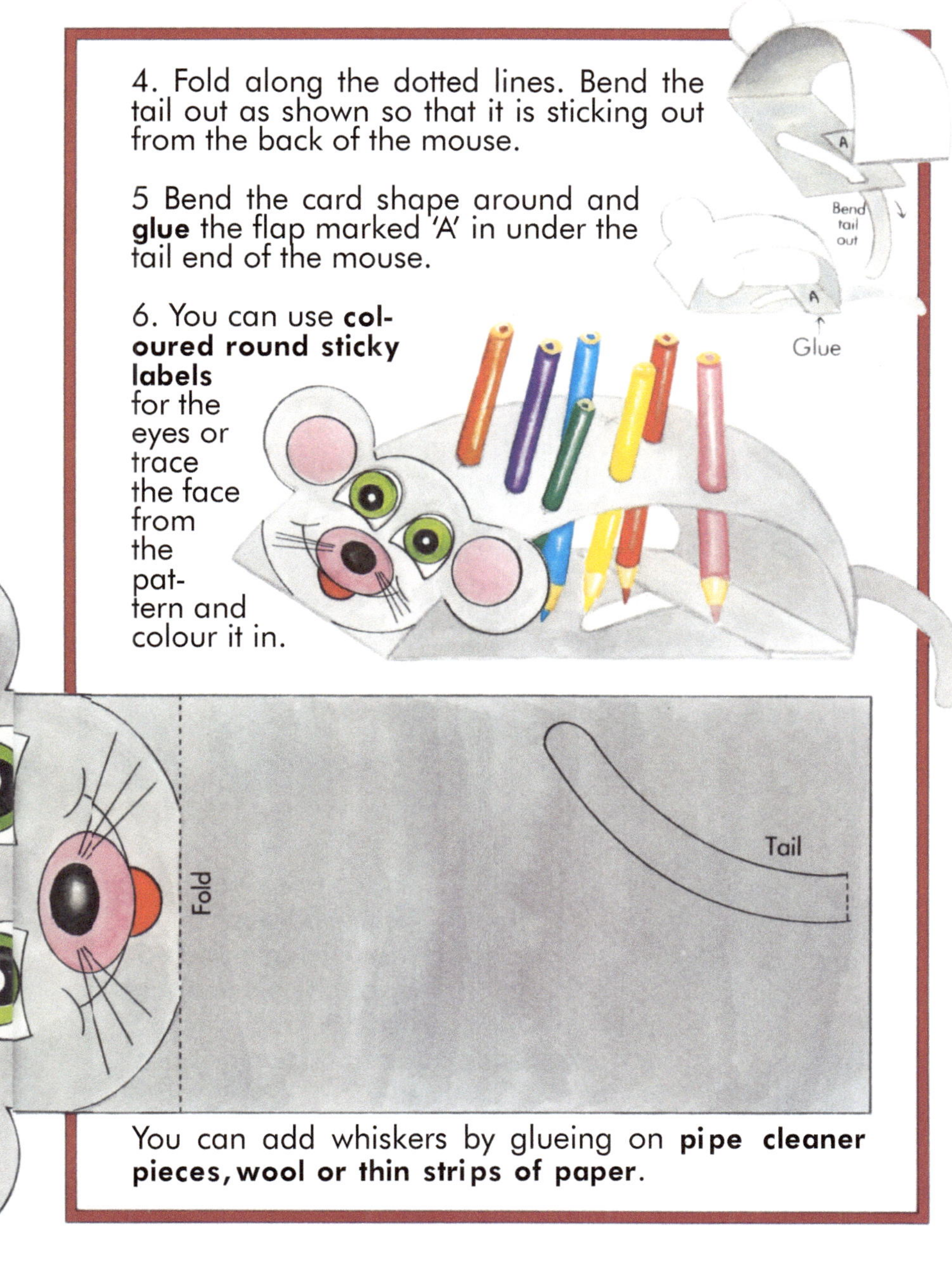

You can add whiskers by glueing on **pipe cleaner pieces, wool or thin strips of paper**.

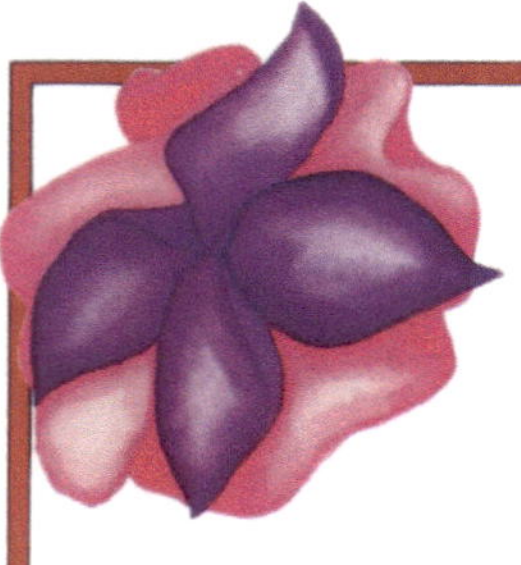

PAPER FLOWER NECKLACE**

The Hawaiians welcome people with necklaces of flowers called leis (lay-ees) and then say 'Aloha' (ah-lo-ha).

You can welcome your friends in the same way by making this paper flower necklace.

1. With scissors cut tissue paper, crepe paper or coloured tissues into squares of different sizes. Fold each square in half, then in half again.

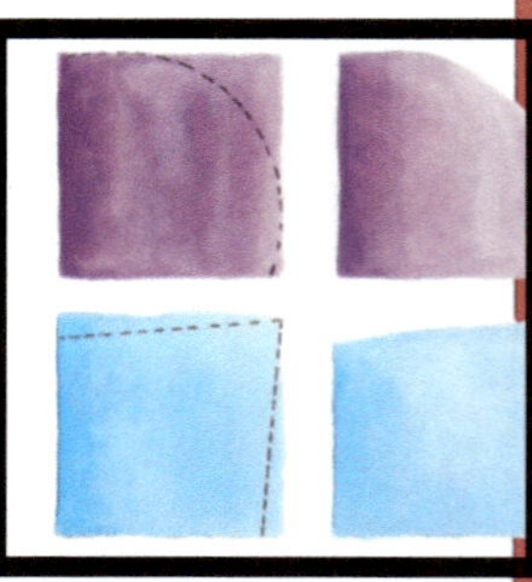

2. Trim around the cut edges of the squares to make some petals curved and others pointed.

3. Hold the pointed end and twist it around. Open out the petals of the flower and lightly stretch the tips and curl them a little.

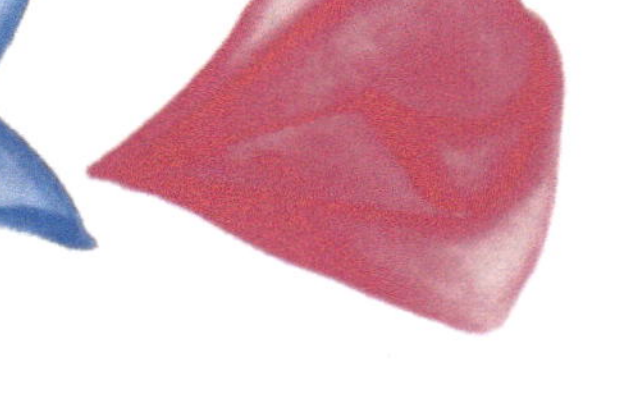

You can also make double flowers. Put two different coloured squares together, fold and cut. Try putting a pointy petalled flower inside a rounded one for a pretty effect.

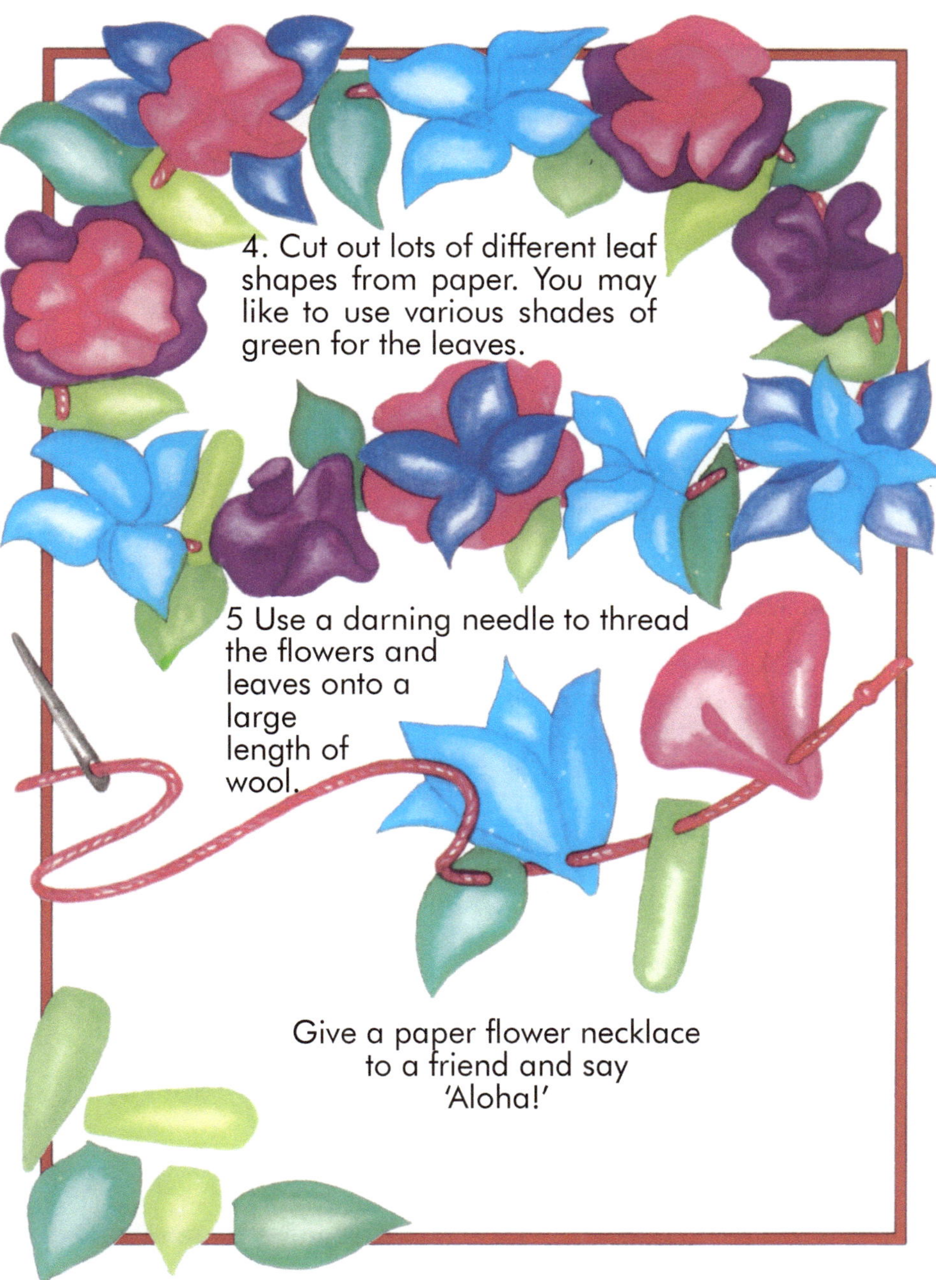

4. Cut out lots of different leaf shapes from paper. You may like to use various shades of green for the leaves.

5 Use a darning needle to thread the flowers and leaves onto a large length of wool.

Give a paper flower necklace to a friend and say 'Aloha!'

MATCHBOX CHEST**

Here is an ideal way to store those tiny things — in a matchbox chest.

1. Take the inside drawer of one matchbox and place it on its end on a sheet of plain coloured or patterned wrapping paper. On the wrong side of the paper, draw around it six times with a pencil.

Use scissors to cut out the shapes.

2. Stick the paper shapes with glue to the fronts of six matchbox drawers.

To make the handles, you will need six brass paper-fasteners. Push them through the front of each one.

Glue

3. Lay the matchboxes side by side in pairs and glue the sides together.

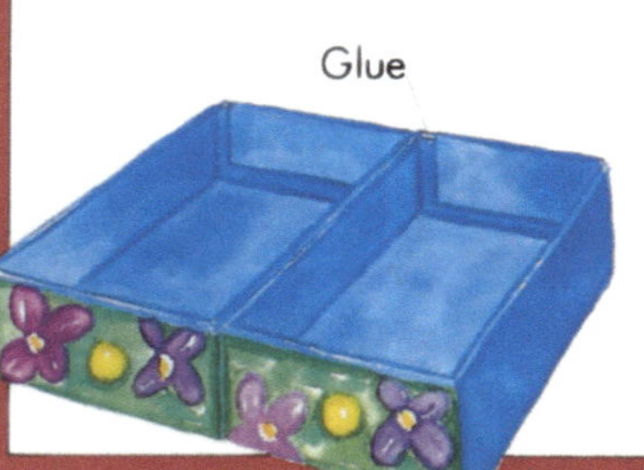

Place the three pairs on top of one another and glue them in place.

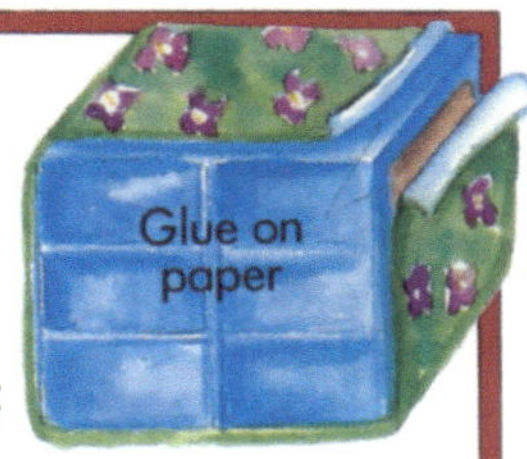

4. With a ruler, measure the sides, top and bottom of the chest and cut a strip of paper to iust over this size.

Coat the chest with glue and wrap the paper around the chest carefully.

If you have used plain paper rather than patterned wrapping paper, decorate the chest with poster paints or markers.

Or you could use pictures cut out of old magazines or greeting cards.

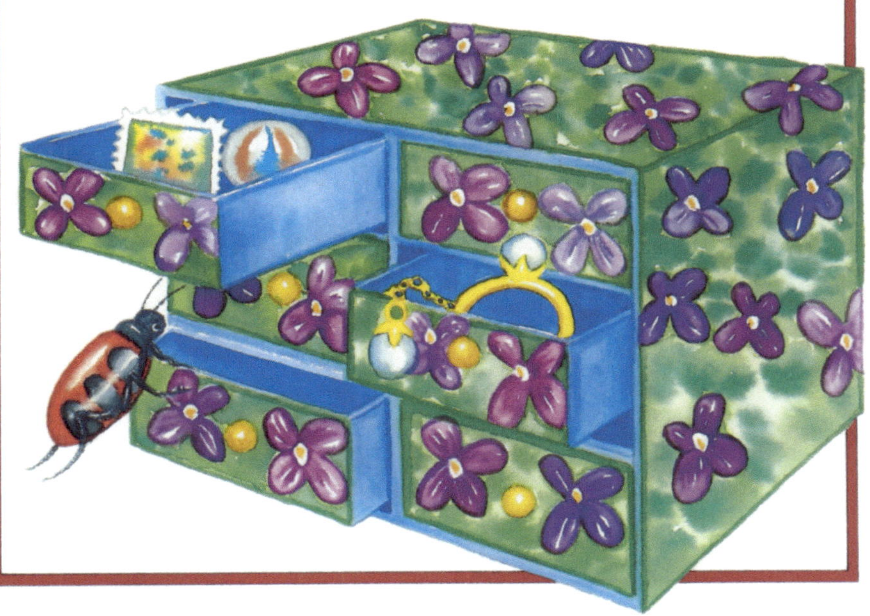

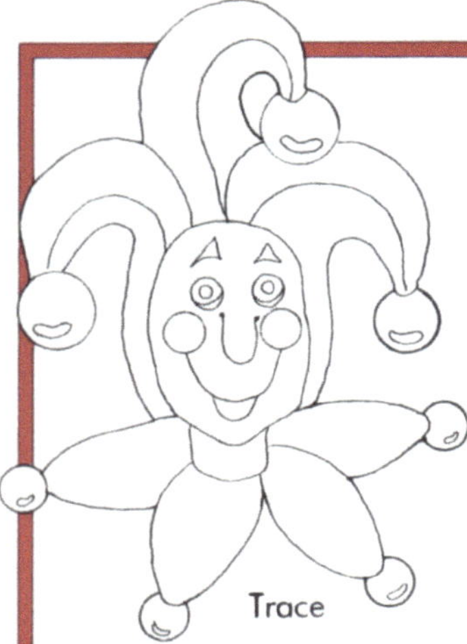

DANCING PUPPET**

Here is a cheerful fellow to make on a rainy day.

1. Trace this head pattern onto **cardboard.** Cut it out and colour it in with **felt-tipped pens.**

Or you can make up your own puppet face.

2. Trace the arm and leg patterns. Using **scissors,** cut two of each out of **felt fabric**. Using **glue or sticky tape**, fix the arms to the sides of **a matchbox** near the top. Fix the legs to the back of the box at the bottom.

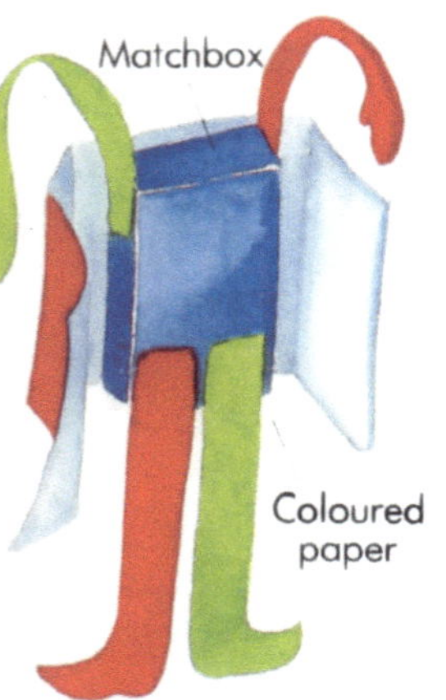

3. Measure around all sides of the box and cut a **strip of paper** to your measurements.

Glue the strip of paper so that it sticks around the box. Use **coloured paper** or **paint** the paper if it is plain.

4. Cut and glue circles of **felt** for paper pom poms on the shoes and body.

Glue the head on to the front of the box, near the top.

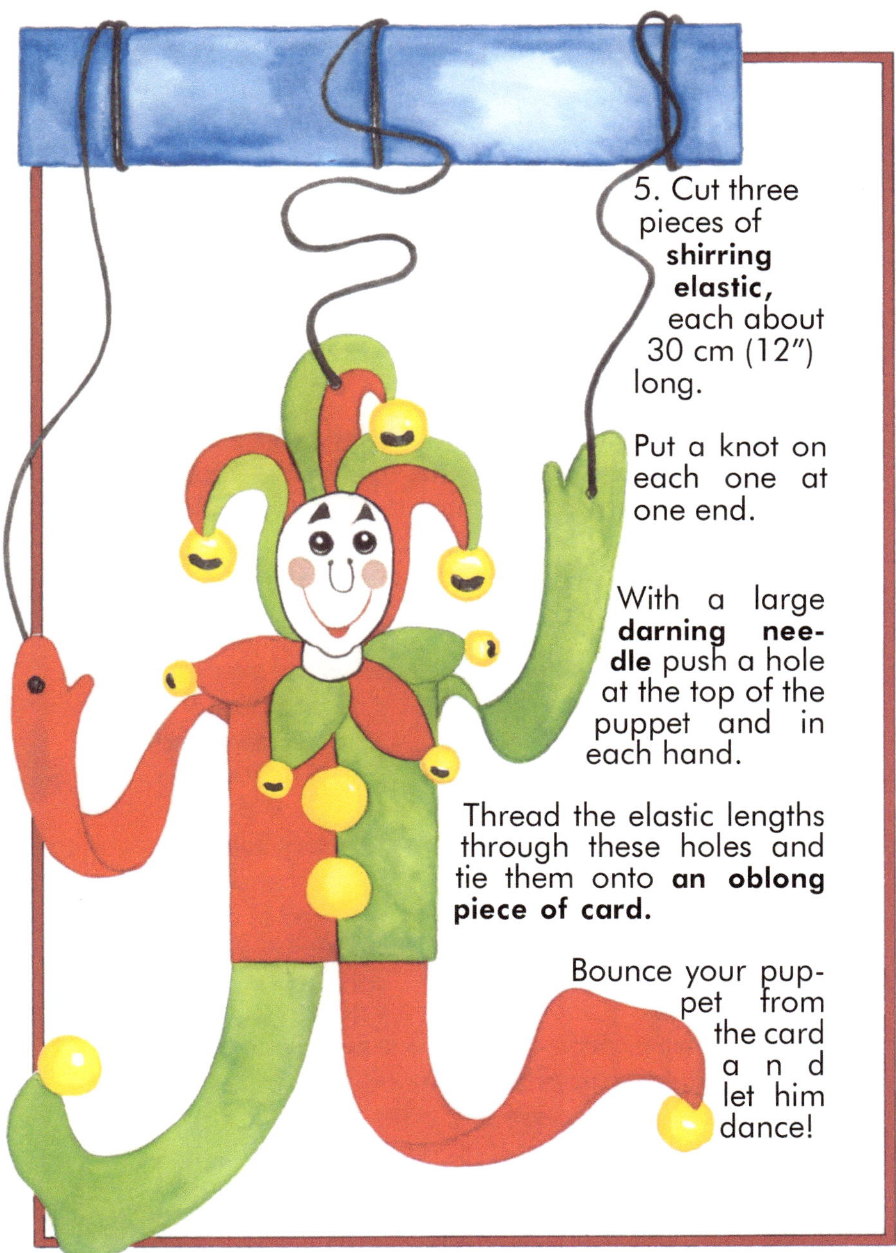

5. Cut three pieces of **shirring elastic,** each about 30 cm (12″) long.

Put a knot on each one at one end.

With a large **darning needle** push a hole at the top of the puppet and in each hand.

Thread the elastic lengths through these holes and tie them onto **an oblong piece of card.**

Bounce your puppet from the card and let him dance!

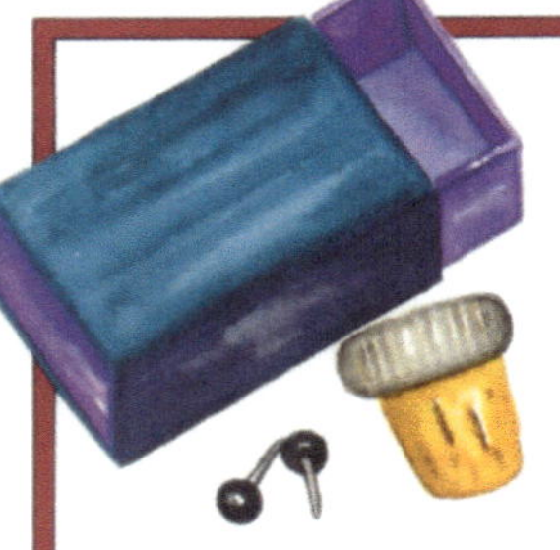

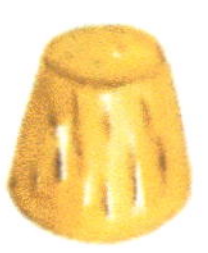

PECKING BIRD**

This colourful bird will peck for food at the touch of your finger.

Find **a large plain cork, a smaller plastic-topped cork and a matchbox**.

Using **a brush**, paint them with **poster paints**.

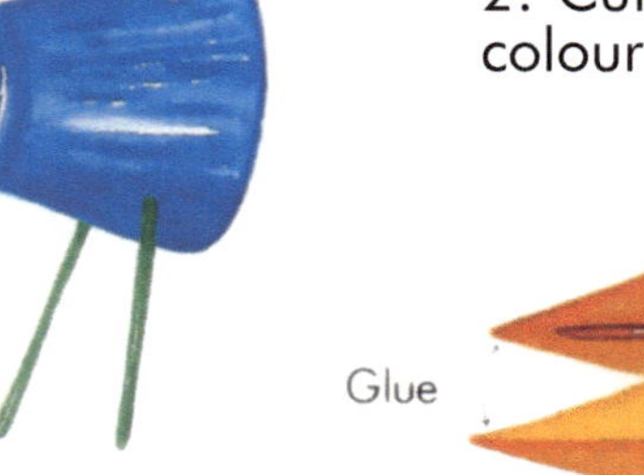

Push **three plastic toothpicks** into the large cork to make the bird's legs and neck. Make sure they fit tightly. Push the plastic-topped cork onto the neck to make the head.

2. Cut two beak shapes out of **paper**, colour and outline as shown.

Glue the two beak shapes together on either side of one end of a **toothpick**.

Push the other end of the toothpick into the front of the plastic-topped cork.

3. Paint a white circle on either side of the cork for the eyes. Push in a **map pin** in each circle to complete the eye.

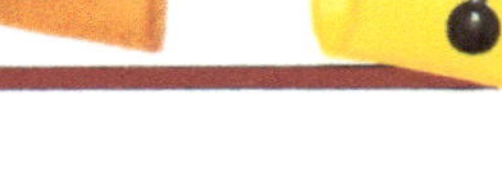

4. Find some **feathers** for the taiL Make holes for them with a tooth-pick. Dab the ends of the feathers with **glue** to secure them.

5. Using this shape (on the right) as a guide for the wings, cut out two pieces and glue them onto the body.

6. Turn the matchbox upside down and push the bird's legs through the box and drawer.

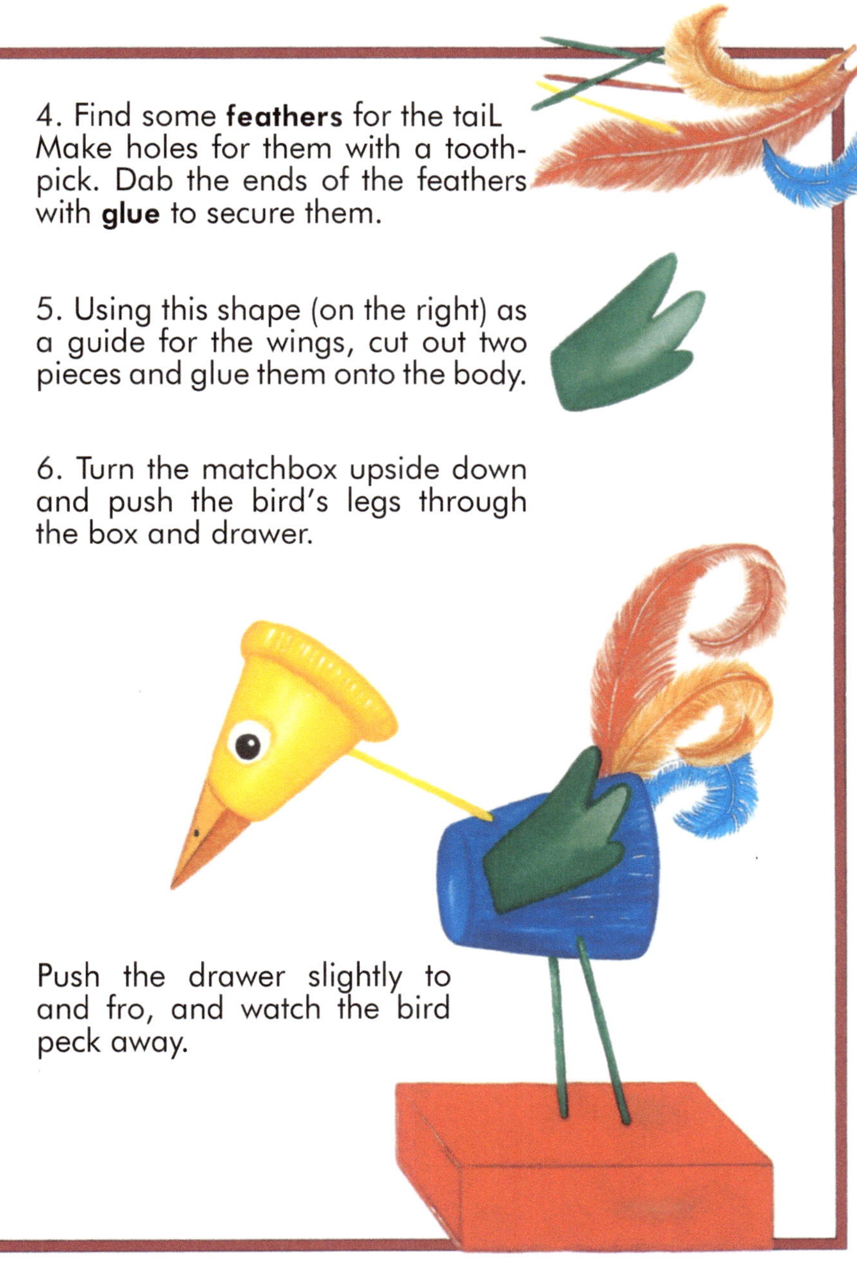

Push the drawer slightly to and fro, and watch the bird peck away.

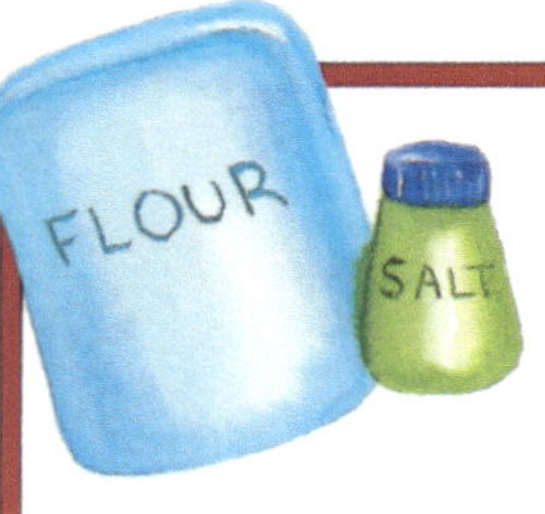

BAKE-A-FRAME ***

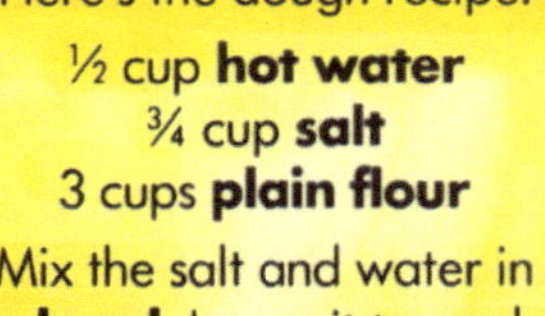

Here's the dough recipe:

½ cup **hot water**
¾ cup **salt**
3 cups **plain flour**

Mix the salt and water in a **bowl**. Leave it to cool. Mix in the flour with your hands working quickly as dough goes brittle.

This picture frame is only for looking at, not for eating! Ask an adult to help you cook it.

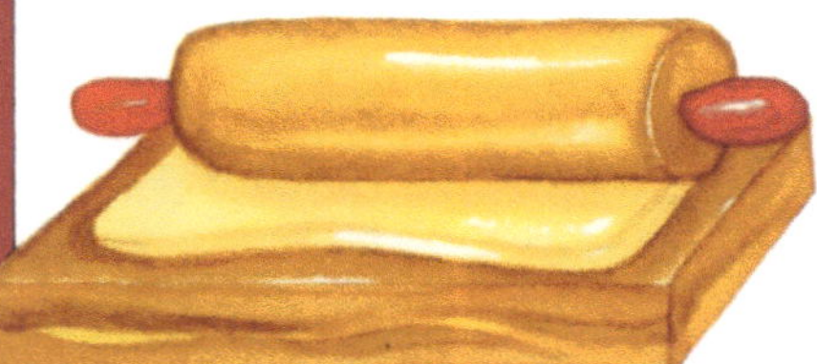

1. Use a **rolling pin** to roll out the dough until it is 1cm (1/2 inch) thick. Trim it to a square with a **kitchen knife** (ask an adult to help) and keep the leftover scraps.

2. Centre **a picture** on the square. Make an outline around the picture lightly with a **wooden skewer or the tip of a blunt knife,** making the outline a little larger than the picture.

3. Using your fingers press inside the outline to make a slight hollow. This is where you will be able to sit your picture when the frame has been cooked.

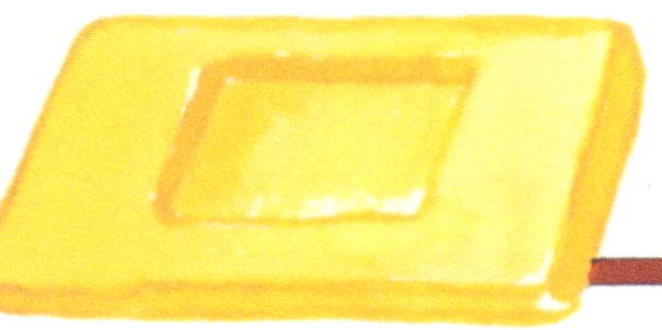

4. Roll and cut the dough scraps into little balls, thin sausages, and other shapes.

Dab the back of the shapes with a little water and press them lightly onto the dough frame. Cook the frame until dry: 30-40 minutes in an oven set at 190° Celsius (375° F).

5. Paint your frame when cool with acrylic paints and glue your picture in the hollow. You may also like to varnish the frame for a shiny finish.

Glue picture in hollow.

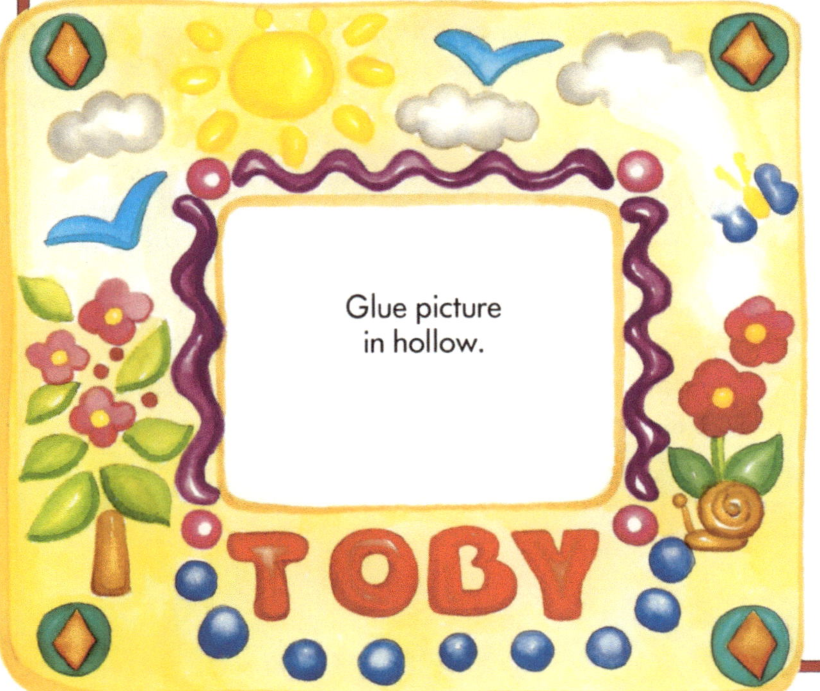

Leaves of Gold Press publishes international, premium quality fiction and non-fiction in hardcover, paperback and ebook format. Our books are printed on high grade, acid-free, book-grade, opaque paper stock sourced from responsibly managed forests.

Our printers are certified by the Forest Stewardship Council™, the Sustainable Forestry Initiative® and the Programme for the Endorsement of Forest Certification™.

Utilizing POD technology reduces paper waste, thereby cutting down greenhouse emissions and conserving valuable natural resources.

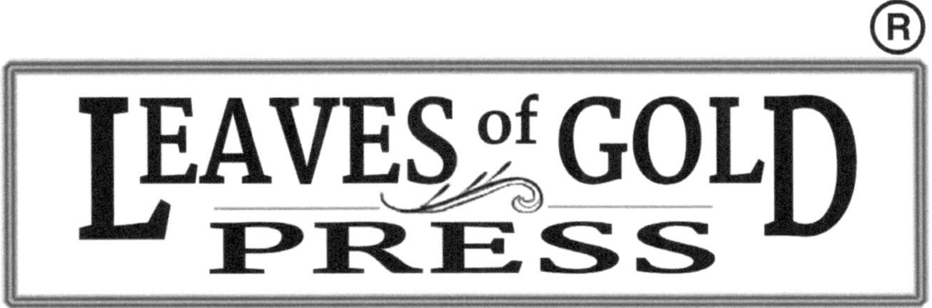

The best books for children, young adults and adults.

www.leavesofgoldpress.com

The 'Parents' Time Off' Series

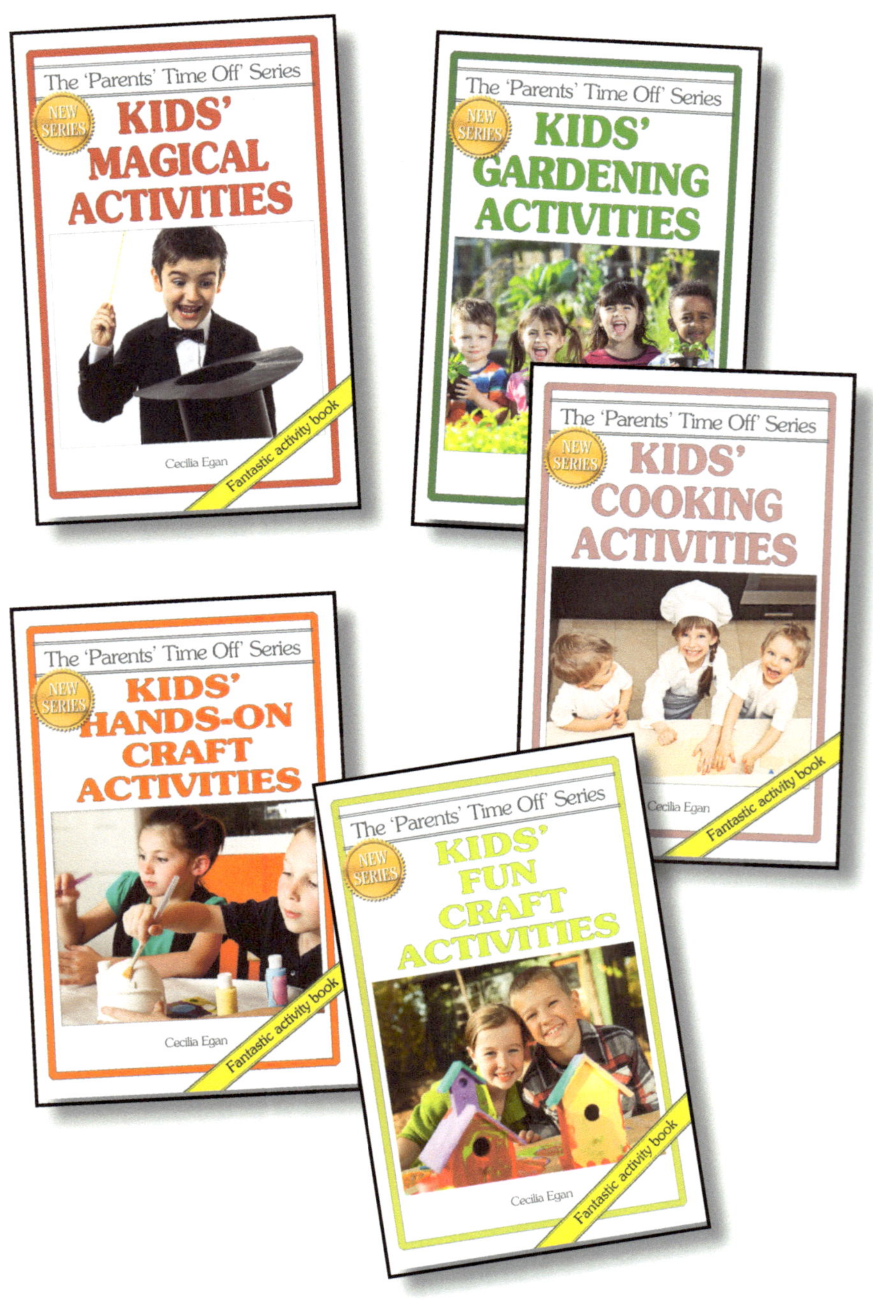

Fantastic activity books — no more school holiday boredom!

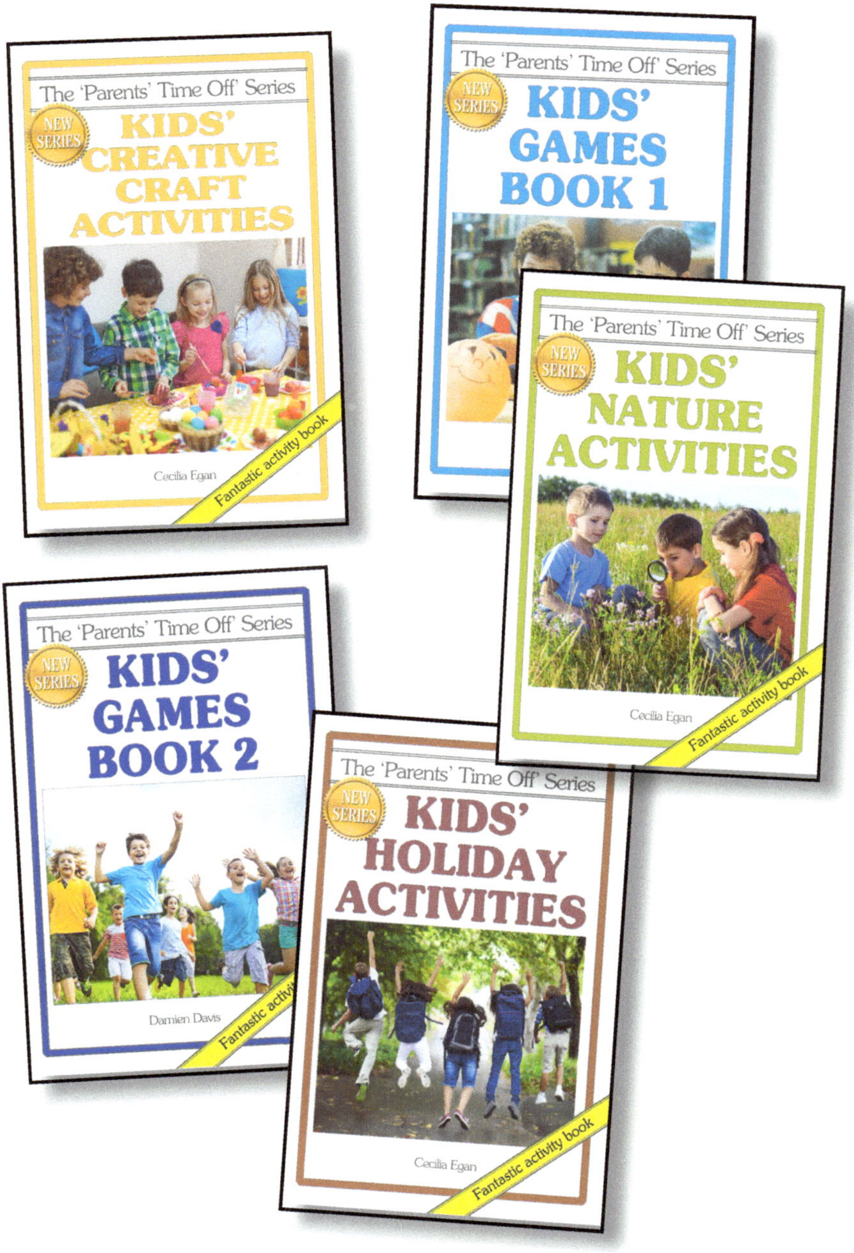

Princess Pam Fell Into the Jam

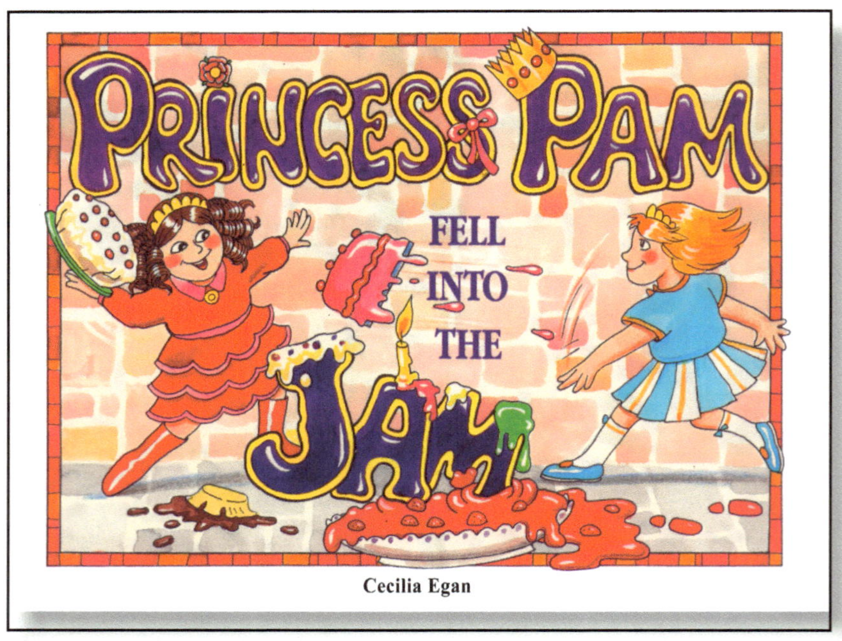

More than a hilarious rhyme, this is a slapstick comedy that causes a riot of laughter when read aloud. Princess Pam and her messy sisters appeal to every child.

The rollicking rhymes, the unconventional story and the lively, detailed pictures combine to make one of the funniest and most original children's books published.

Princess Pam and the Twenty-eight Brave Princes

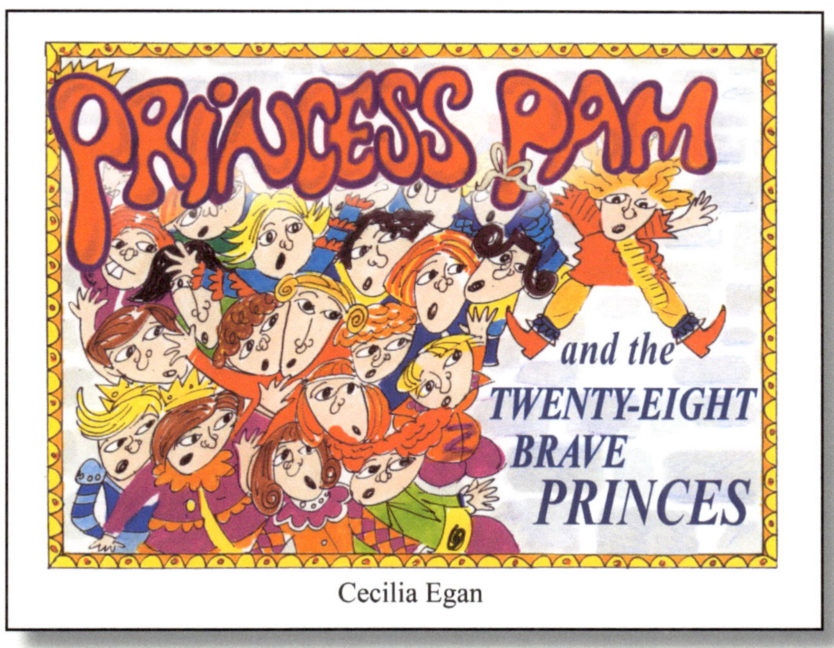

In this, the second in the riotous "Princess Pam" series, Princess Pam becomes involved in more uproarious, slapstick comedy when she and her naughty sisters and cousins meet the Brave Princes.

Classic Fairytales from Tolkien's Bookshelf

- Grimms' Fairytales - Illustrated
- The Red Fairy Book - Illustrated
- The Princess and the Goblin - Illustrated.
- The Story of King Arthur and his Knights - Illustrated

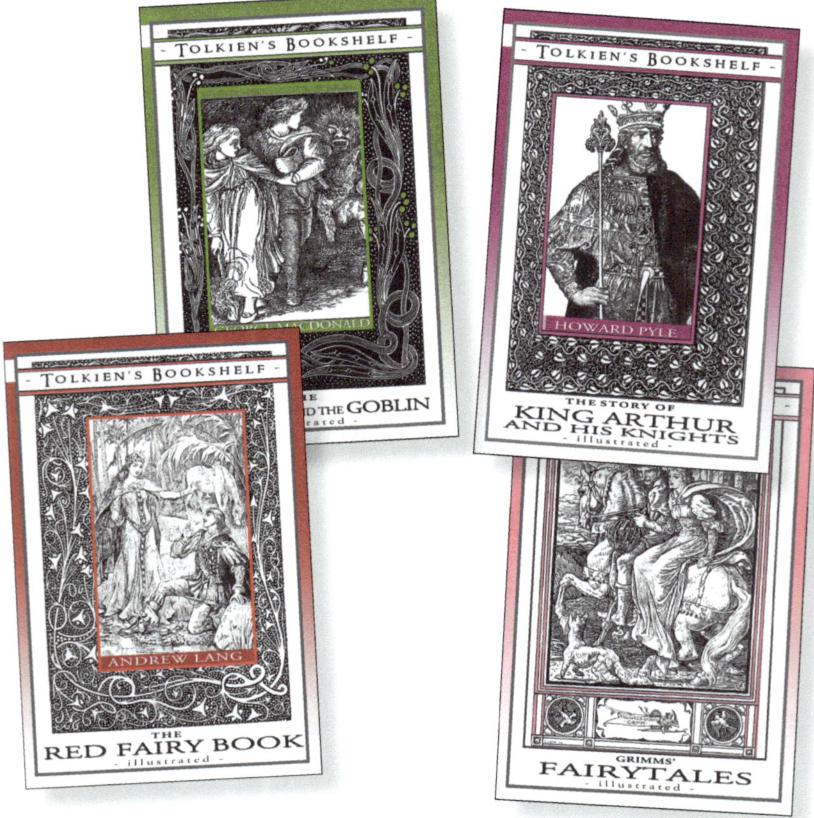

Find out more on our website!

www.leavesofgoldpress.com

The Fairytale Sequels

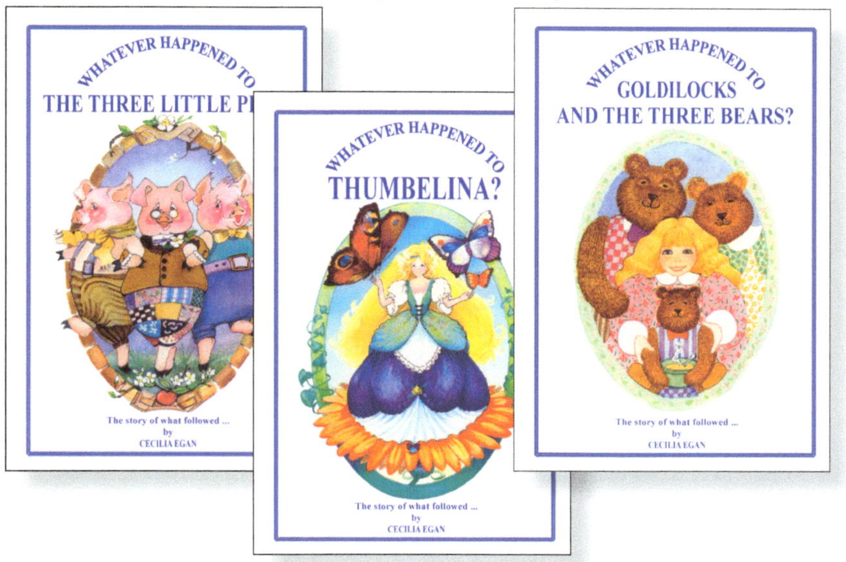

The Nursery Rhyme Stories

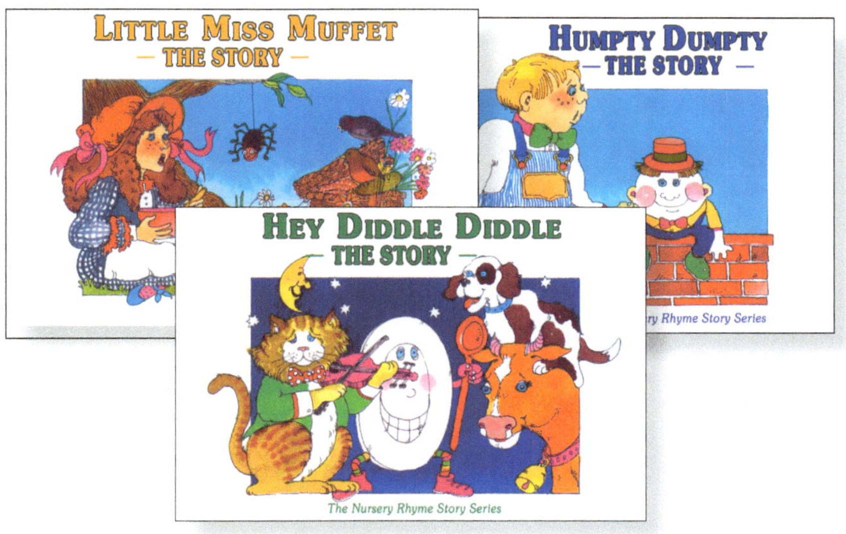

www.ingramcontent.com/pod-product-compliance
Lightning Source LLC
LaVergne TN
LVHW052301100826
845147LV00001B/106

9781925110739